MW01628226

Love, Jan

Jan Sitts

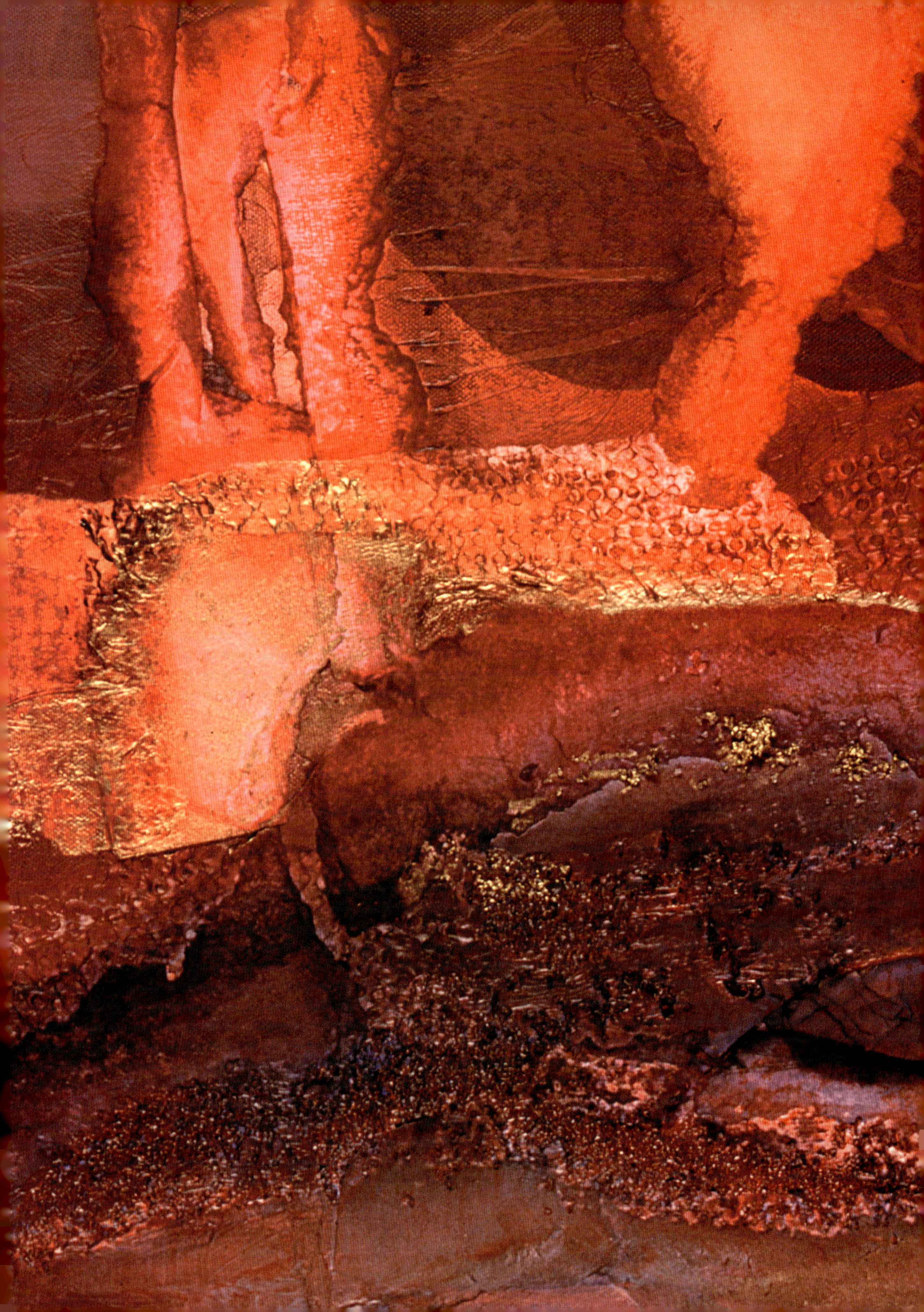

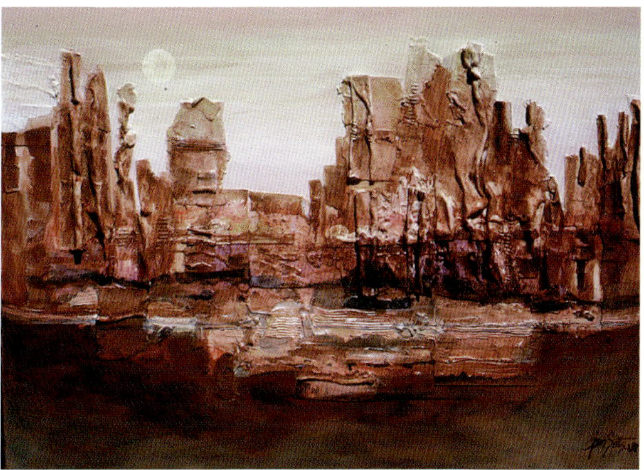

TextureColorFeeling

Many techniques, materials, approaches to composition, and, above all, emotions, play off of each other when I am creating a piece. By combining aggressive textures, unusual media, and various raw materials, I work toward an end result which is the creative accomplishment of the painting. I am attracted to mixed media for its endless possibilities. The adventure lies in not knowing where you are going — until you get there!

Mixed media and exploratory techniques are not the terrain of the traditional painter, but students who journey with me experience a "visual sensation" throughout the process if they are able and willing to let go of old habits, break the paradigm. Beginning the journey in mixed media requires an understanding of painting, mixing and layering colors, executing shapes by working with positive and negative space, and nurturing an affinity for texture. Once armed with a knowledge of the fundamentals and of the possibilities of various media, creative spontaneity comes naturally. This continuous process of sustaining, validating, and then reinventing is part of cultivating the creativity that nurtures our souls as food does our physical beings.

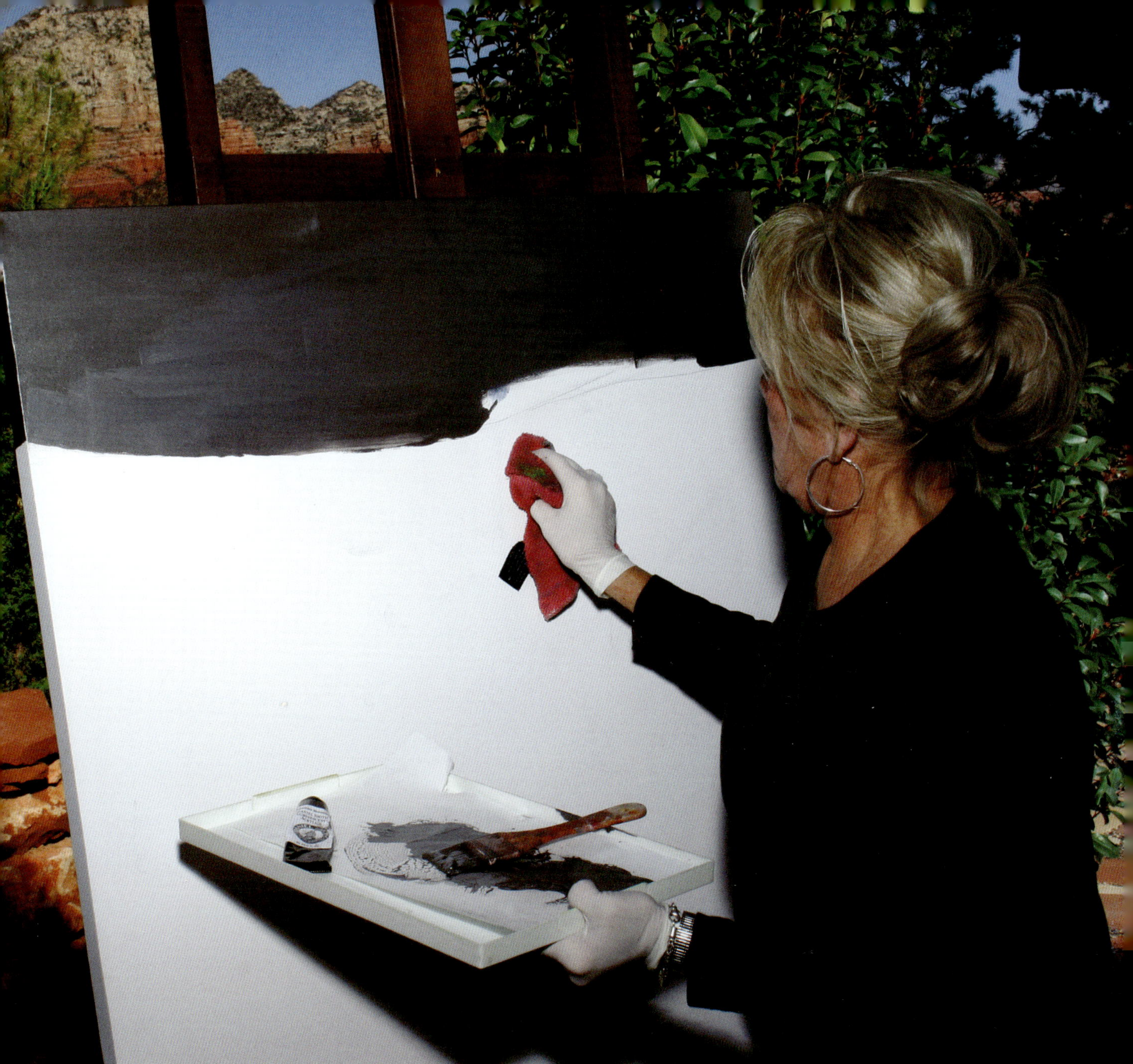

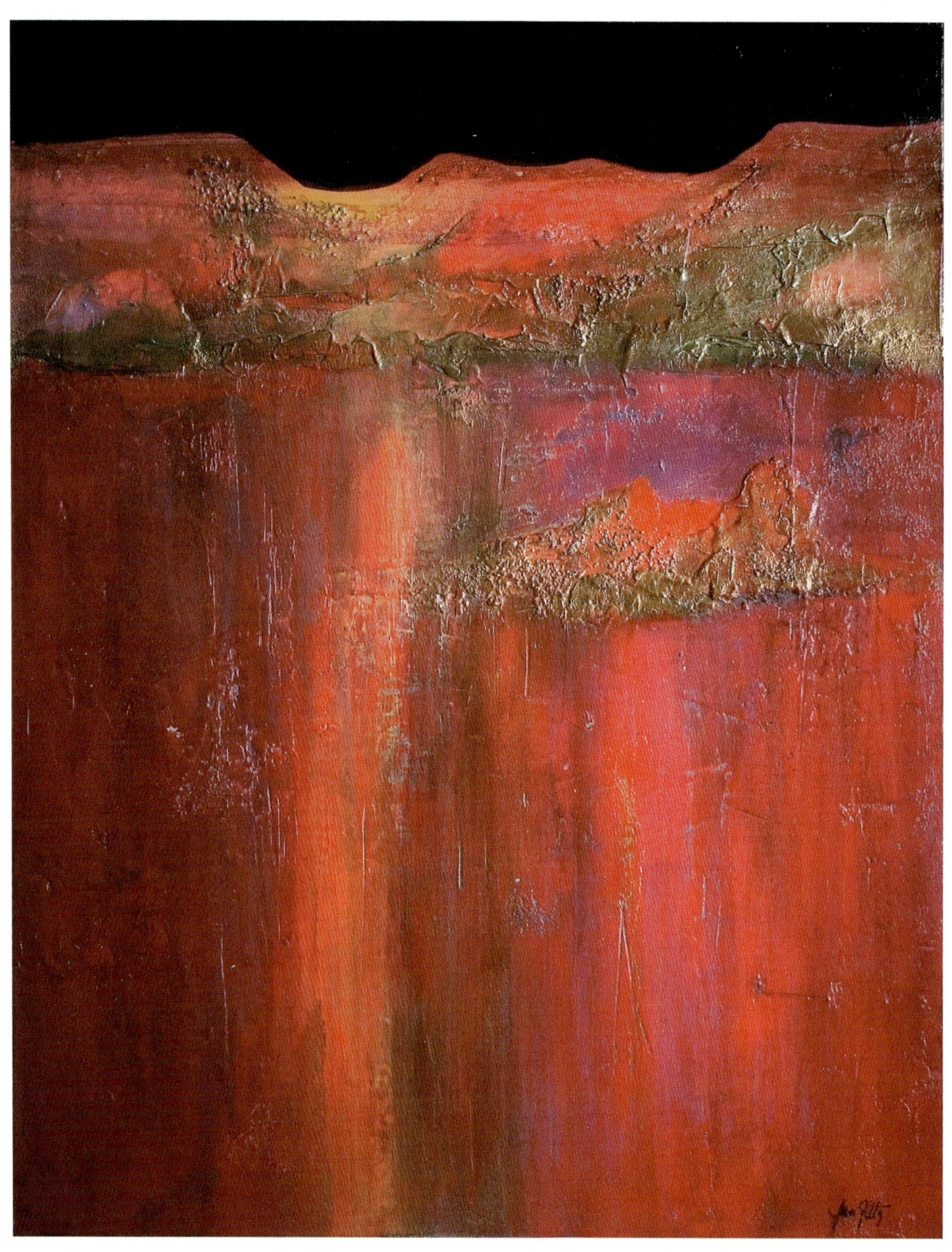

SOUTHWEST LANDMARKS

24 x 30, mixed media

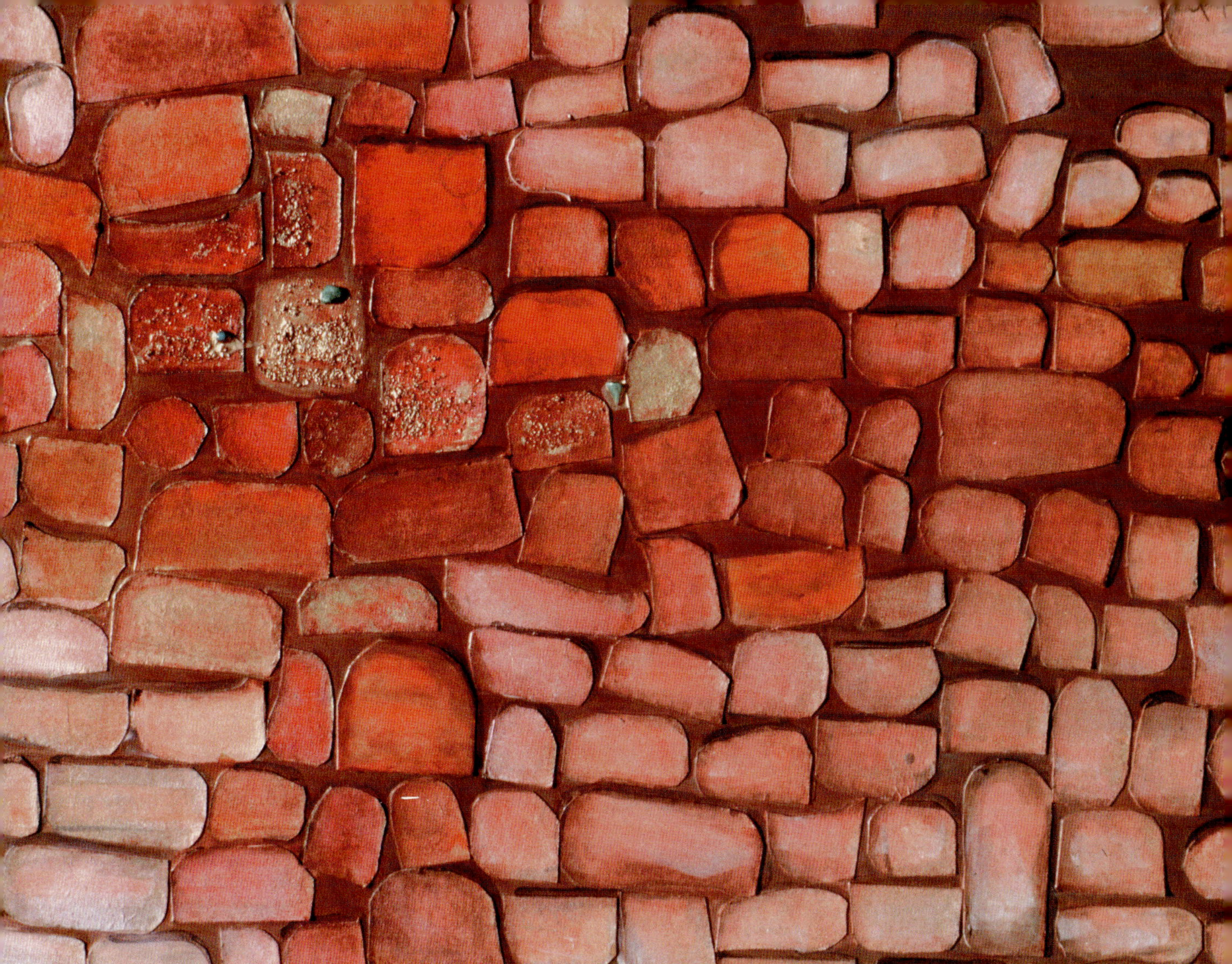

Through the years I have experimented with all the design formats that were available to me, and the design I have come to favor over all others is the cruciform. I have used this design in creating complex compositions through layering paper and exploring form with color and texture. I have always felt that my spirituality plays an important part in my life's work and I want to express this in my paintings. One of my collectors responded to this design by saying, "The painting touched me deeply as in one strike of lightning I saw in the cross a symbol of every human life." This simple but complex design format has led me to the "heart-and-hand" core of my work.

REDSTONES
36 x 48, mixed media on canvas

Abstracting the landscape of Sedona by cutting out individual paper pieces and applying them to the canvas gave me the effect of "red stones." The illuminated red rock formations of the area produce a breathtakingly theatrical scene.

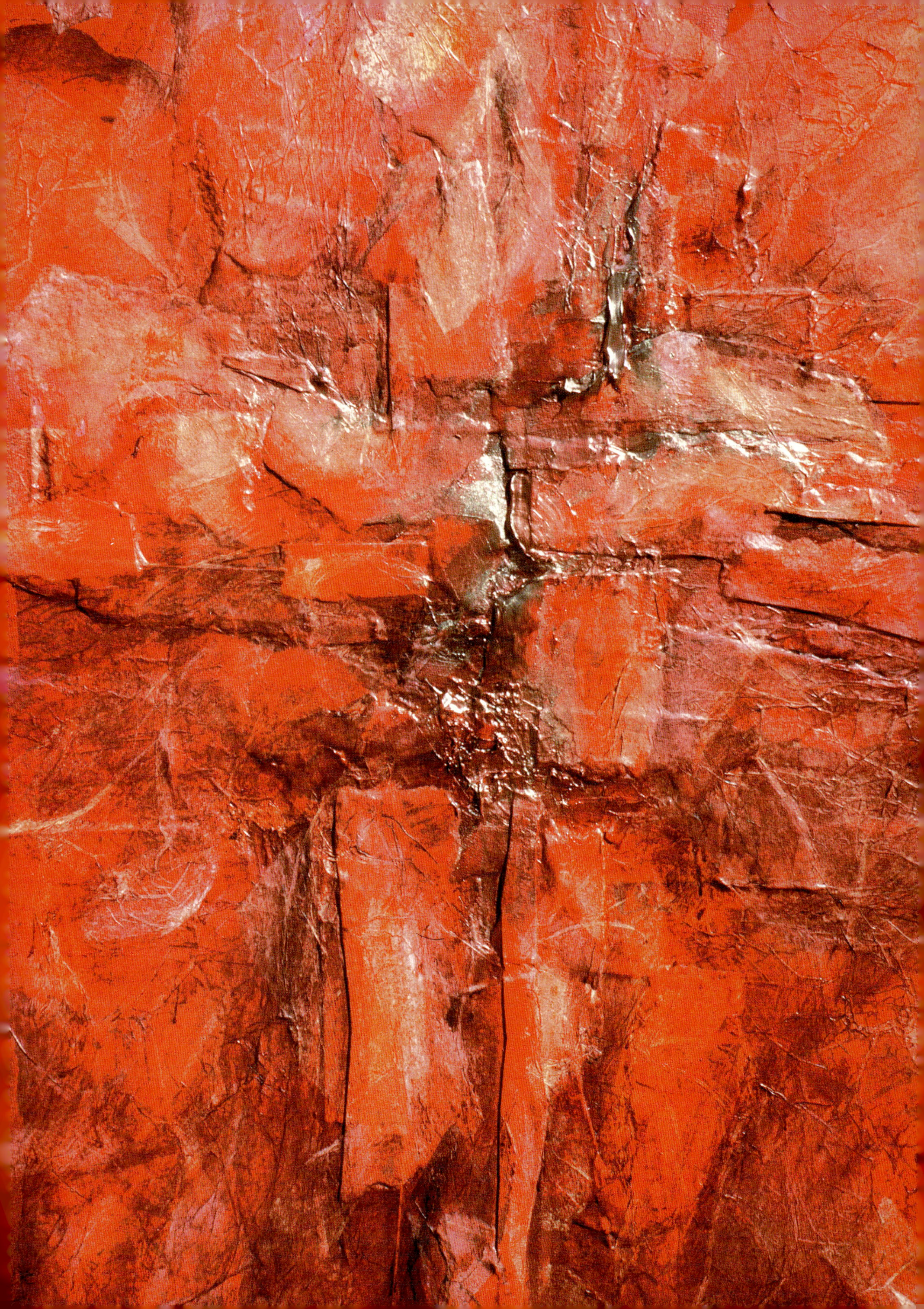

When I am demonstrating varied techniques, the lessons evolve from simple tasks such as preparing the papers — folding, crumpling, pleating, tearing, and cutting — to the layering of color.

The work starts with all-white acid-free papers, which provide luminescent layers for the later addition of warm and cool paint choices. The support surface always remains white and textured until I begin painting. From this beginning, I can expand the painting through a variety of materials on a variety of surfaces while responding to the outcome as an idea. This idea may be a process that will be carried from one painting to the next. Each time I paint, something is added through layering papers, mediums, and textures. If the outcome of the process becomes predictable, I move on to another sequence or approach. Seldom do I begin with a conscious idea. The idea emerges as the painting evolves.

After the art piece is totally completed, I use a good ultraviolet light-protective polymer spray varnish in matte or gloss. I spray several coats (preferably outdoors.) This polymer is also used in today's frameless artwork for exhibitions. This textural layering technique in mixed media painting is very archival.

Making mixed media artworks is a freeing and joyful way to express my pleasure in the physical world with all its textures and colors. Join me in the following demonstrations of process and technique, and then stroll through the pages of a portfolio gallery.

~ JAN SITTS

SPIRITS OF FIRE

30 x 40, mixed media on canvas

Demonstrating the process: Copper Moon Rising

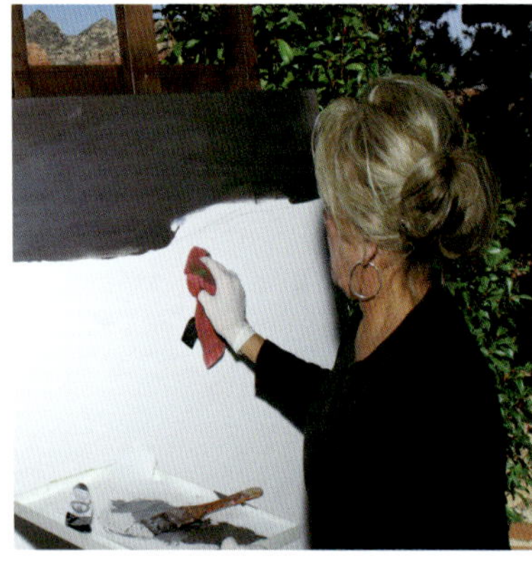

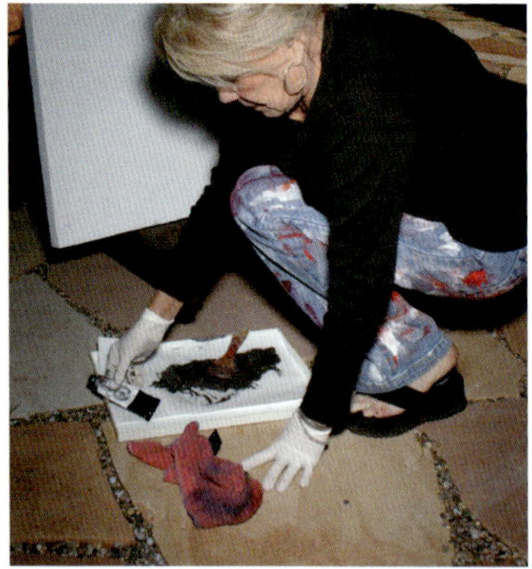

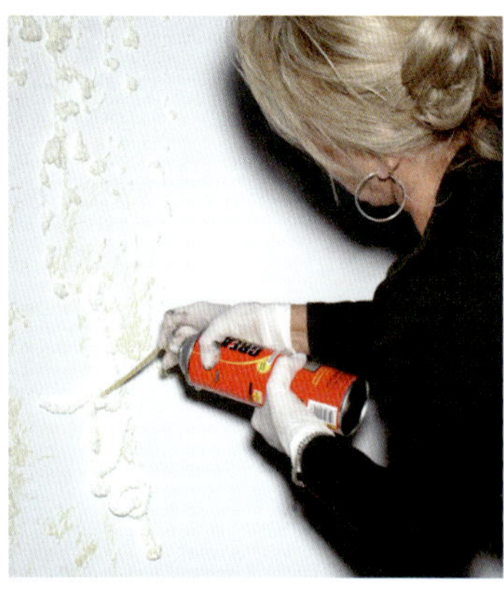

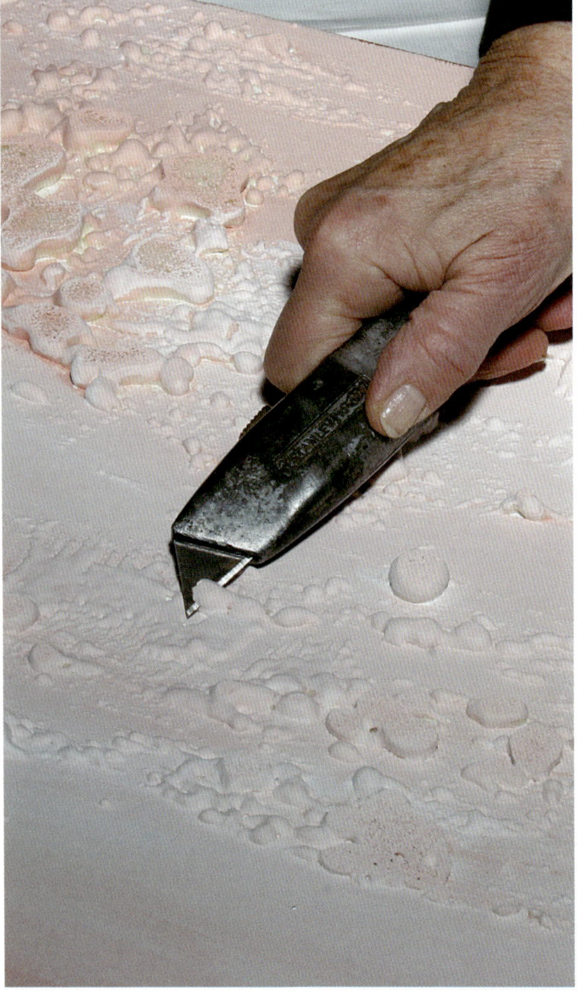

STEP 1: I started this painting outdoors using iridescent moonstone acrylic on the upper portion of the piece. The penciled high horizon line, which was drawn in beforehand, was the guideline for how far down to paint the canvas.

STEP 2: The texture was applied with a can of insulating foam sealant that comes with a plastic screw-on nozzle. This texture was sprayed from the horizon line down over a majority of the canvas. In areas where I wanted more texture, I repeated the process directly over the still-wet initial coating. A three-inch putty knife was used to knock down the texture as I sprayed. The sealant requires twenty-four hours to dry.

STEP 3: When the upper portion of the canvas was dry, I cut out a copper metal circle and applied it to the canvas with spray glue. (The metal cannot be moved once applied, so you need to place it carefully.) I scored the moon to give it texture and enhance light reflection.

STEP 4: Using a sharp utility knife, I carefully sliced off the areas of hardened sealant that were most raised. This is time-consuming and messy but worth it for beautiful textured result. One coat of white gesso was then painted over the worked area.

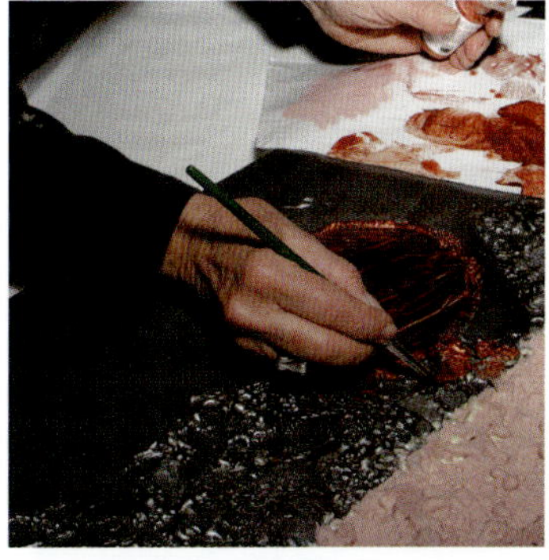

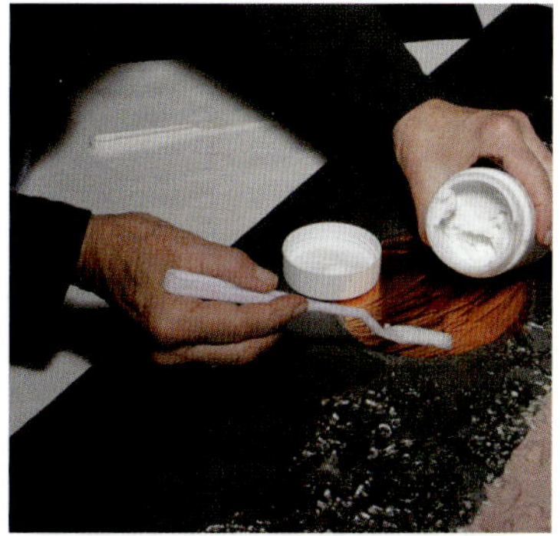

STEP 5: While waiting for the gesso to dry I used a small-tipped palette knife to edge the moon with an acrylic gel of glass beads. I also painted some of the raised texture "bubbles" around the moon in copper and metallic gold.

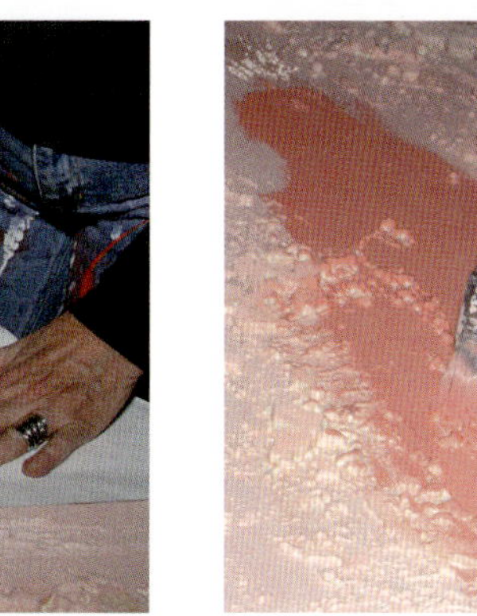

STEP 6: The first layer of paint was a mixture of white gesso, burnt sienna, and a small amount of quinacridone magenta. The middle area of the canvas was painted with vat orange, magenta, and white gesso. After this layer dried, I applied a second layer of metallic gold. When painting on the color, I suggest you use an old brush as you must work in and around the texture "bubbles."

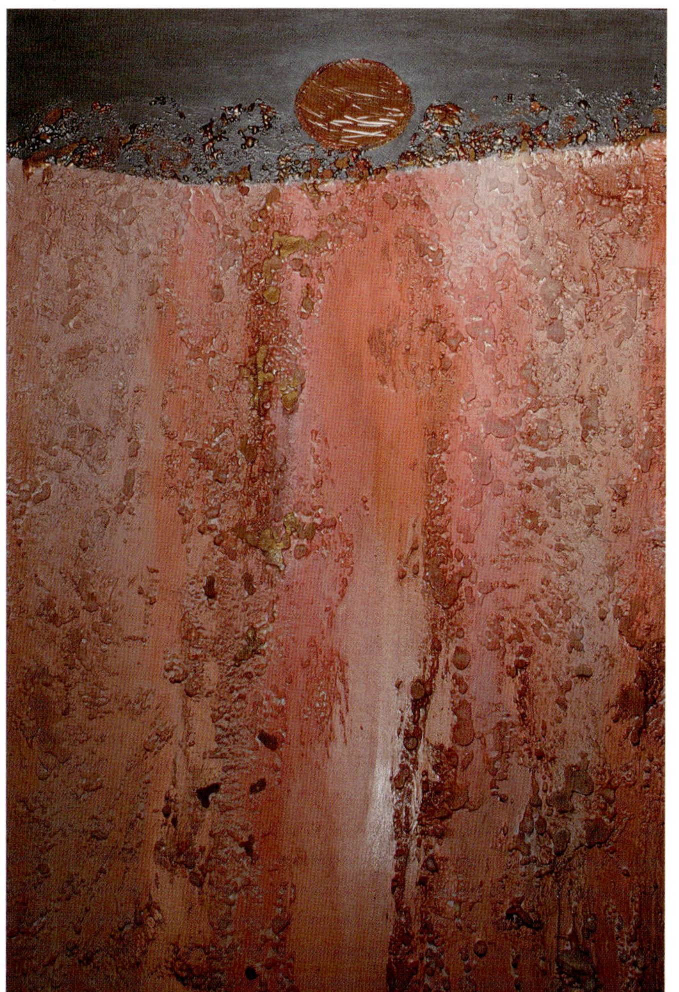

STEP 7: When the canvas was completed, I turned it around frequently and checked for little missing areas I might have forgotten to paint on the heavy textured surface. It is a good idea to save your acrylic paint mixtures in little plastic cups with lids for this final step.

A NOTE ON MATERIALS: Because my husband is a contractor, I find myself going to his workshop and looking for unusual building materials for my mixed-media work. This is how I discovered the possibilities of insulating foam sealant. The sealant has a mind of its own when you begin spraying the canvas — but what fun the spontaneous venture is!

Demonstrating the process: Vibrant Hills

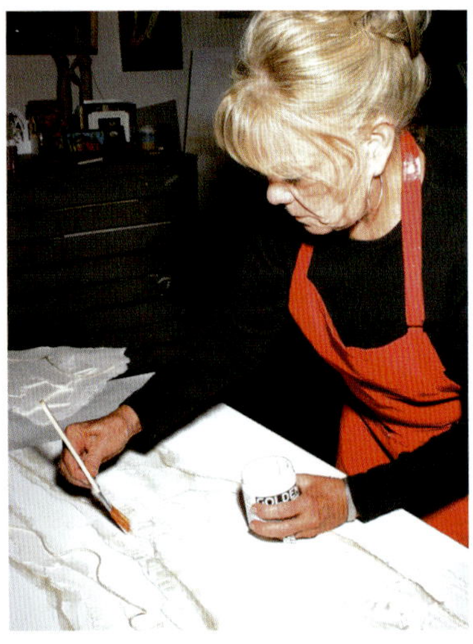

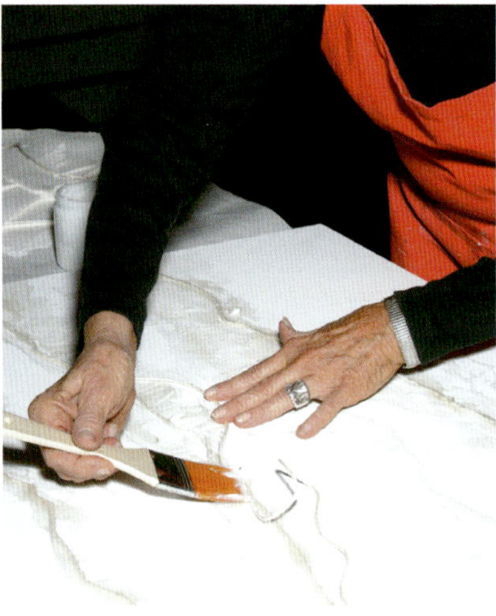

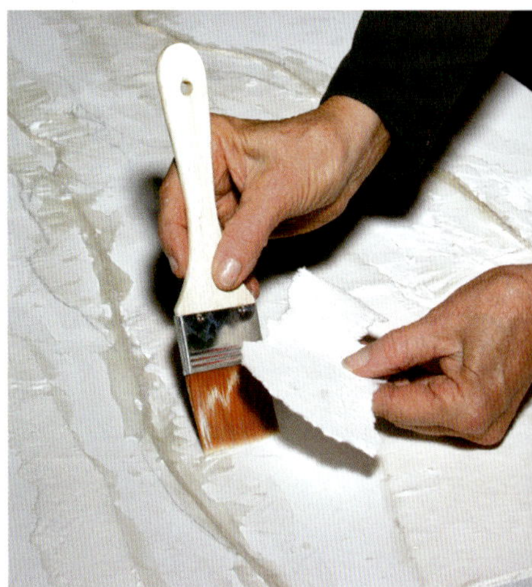

STEP 1: With gel medium and a small palette knife I apply a narrow line to form a landscape of "hills" on my horizontal canvas. The line is drawn spontaneously.

STEP 2: I then carefully lay cotton string over the gel line and gently press it into the medium so it will adhere. I cover some areas of string with extra gel. The canvas is set aside to dry.

STEP 3: I then tear a shape from linter paper, dip it in water, and brush matte medium on its back side so that I can apply it to the canvas surface. I tear various sizes and shapes of linter paper and continue this process spontaneously until I have ample shapes forming a beautiful texture.

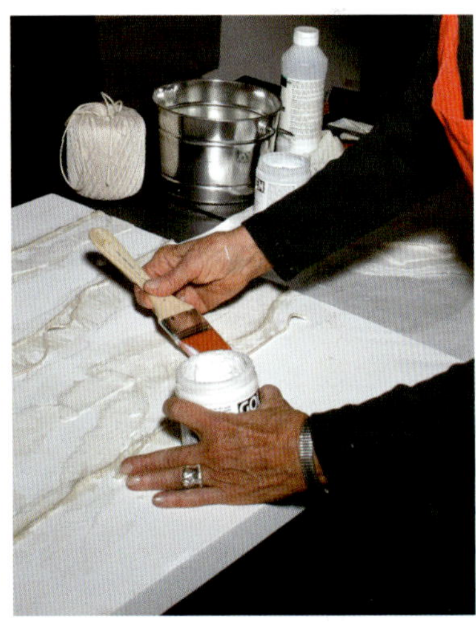

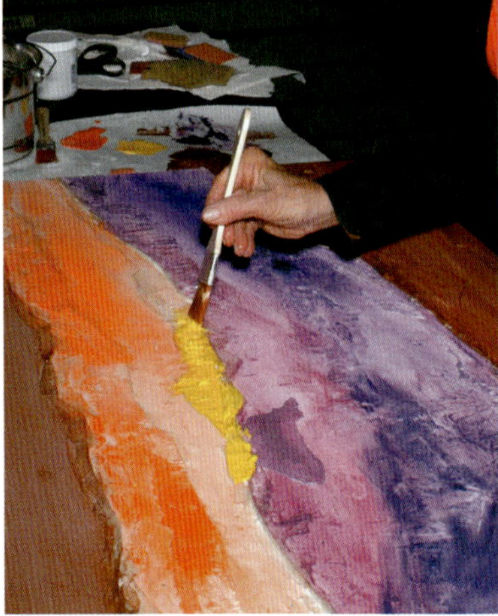

STEP 4: After the cotton linter paper is dry, I apply gel with a palette knife and score the gel to form a grass-like surface. Glass beads are placed in the gel to lead the eye through the composition and create more texture.

STEP 5: I apply opaque and transparent acrylic paint in layers, leaving each layer to dry before the next is added. The color changes with each layer of paint, coming closer to the luminosity I want to achieve.

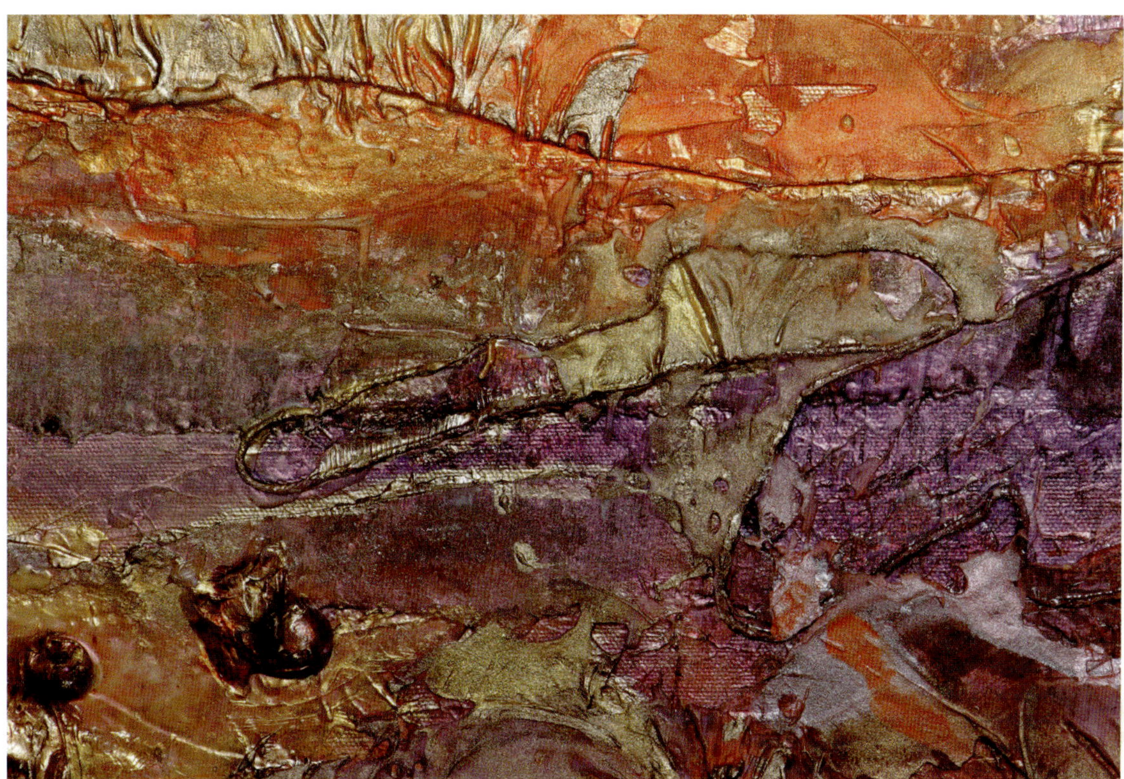

STEP 6: Adding and adjusting the color: The highly textured raised areas or peaks and valleys of the canvas often need additional paint or thickness of color. Subtle adjustments are made with small brushes.

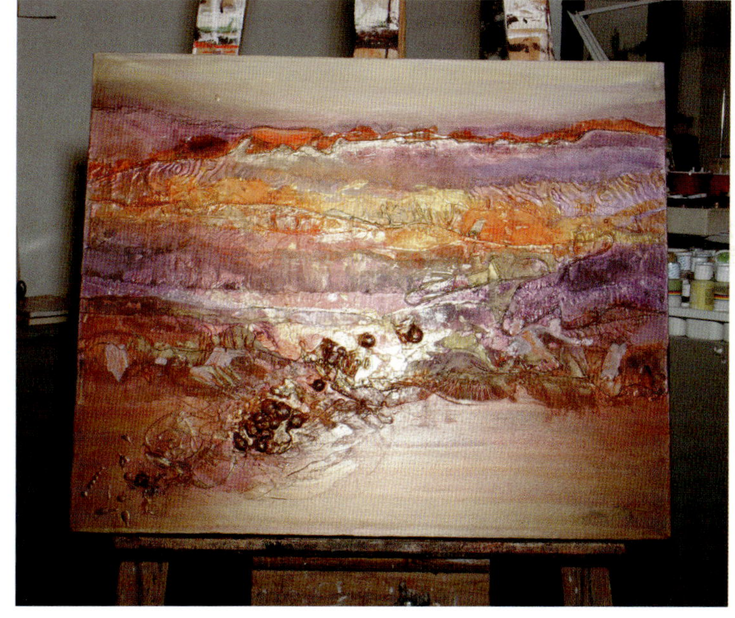

A NOTE ON MATERIALS: It is very important to use full strength matte medium for applying the cotton linter papers, as you are applying them over a highly textured dry surface.

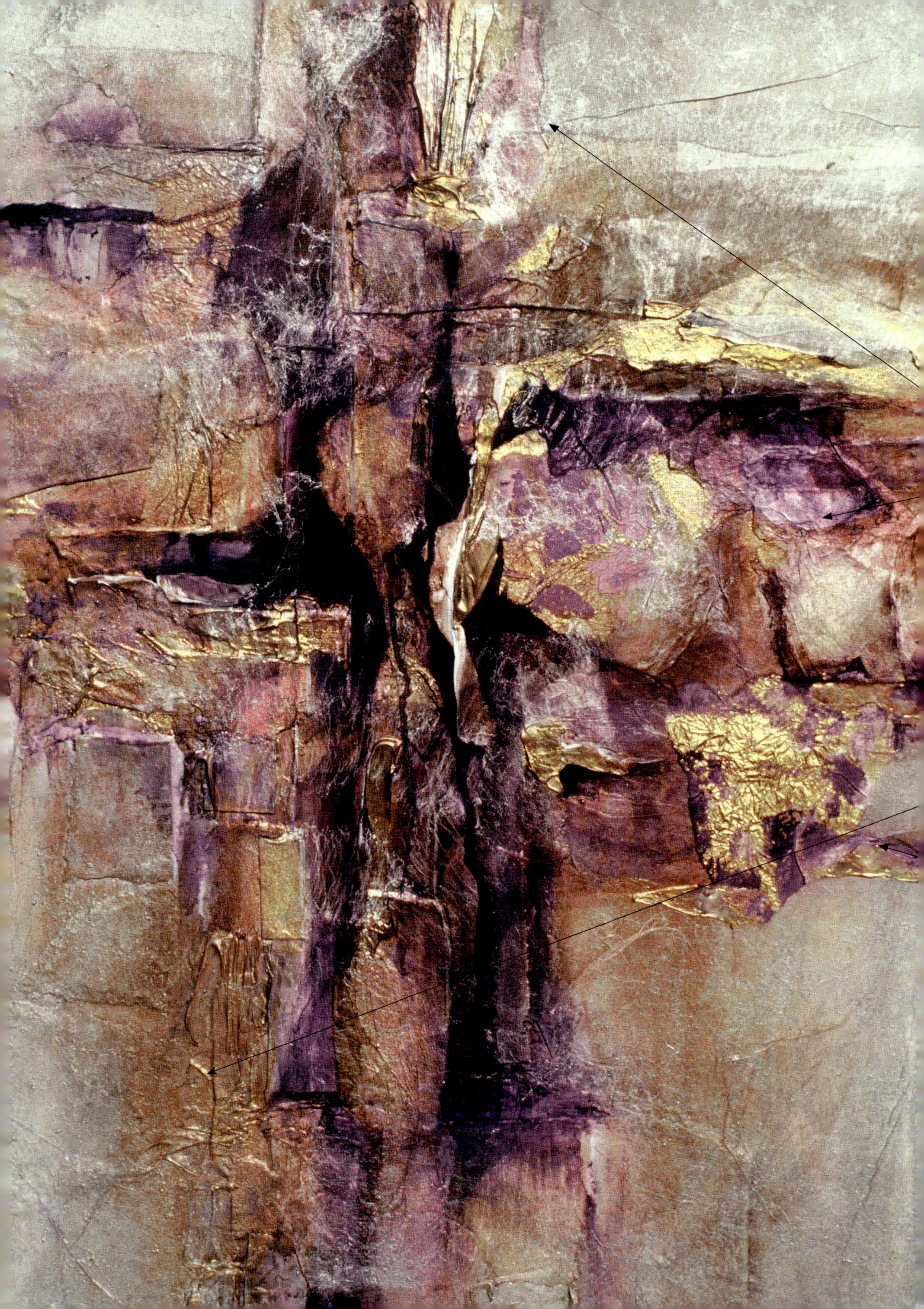

Summary of technique: To Seek a Vision

Heavy, unsized blotter paper was cut and torn in various sizes.

I dipped the paper shapes in water and brushed each one with full-strength acrylic matte medium to adhere it to the raw canvas surface. The shapes were laid onto the canvas in a manner that took on the shape of a cross.

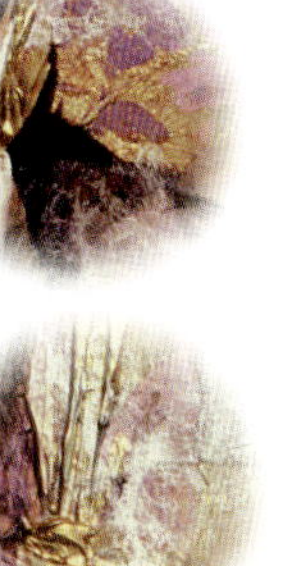

Some smaller shapes were overlapped over larger ones to get a three-dimensional effect and a heavier texture.

I crushed and crinkled Tyvek and applied it to the piece. Tyvek is a sturdy, fibrous material used in making kites. It needs several applications of matte medium — applied both to the canvas and the Tyvek — to make it adhere well.

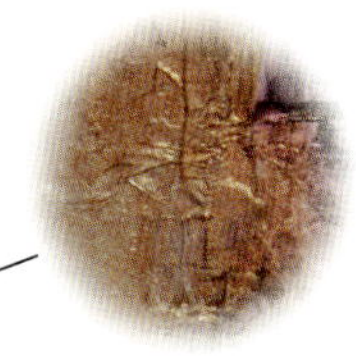

Art tissue was torn into many shapes and applied in the same manner as the Tyvek.

After the piece was completely dry, I painted it spontaneously, using colors that signify spirituality to me: purple, bright silver, pearlescent gold. I painted in the background washes with sepia to bring the other colors forward.

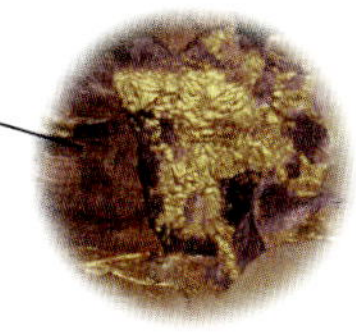

I added small squares of gold leaf, adhered with matte medium. As I pressed the gold leaf into the crevices of the Tyvek I could see an interesting effect emerging.

When the piece was complete, I sprayed it with several coats of UV polymer matte varnish to permanently stabilize the materials.

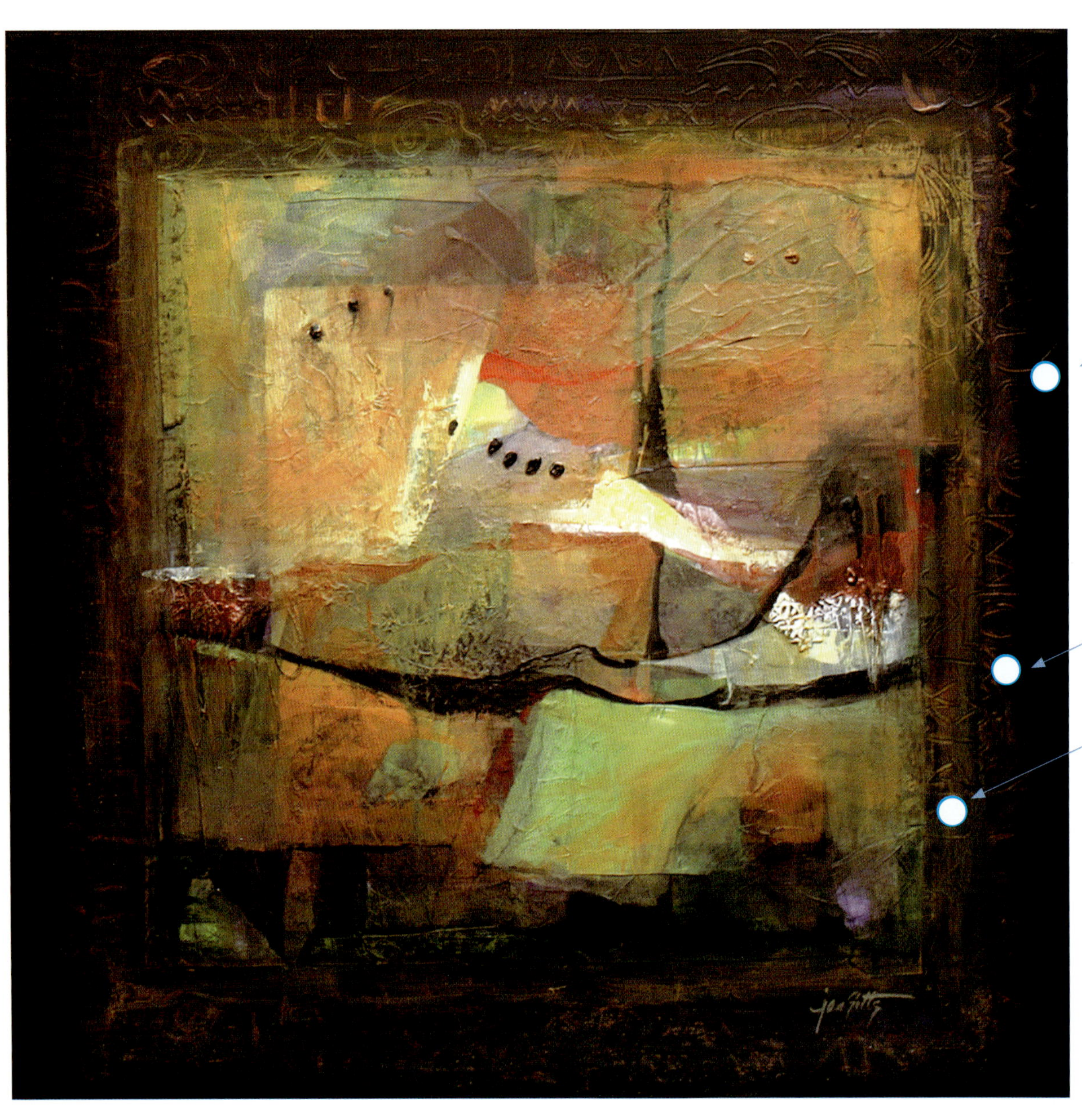

Summary of technique: High Top

The format for this painting is a frame within a frame, and the composition was built around this concept.

A thick coat of gesso was applied around the outer edge of the canvas, about three inches wide. This became the outer frame.

With a brush handle, I carved personal symbols into the wet gesso around the entire piece.

Over the dried gesso, I painted a deep violet frame . . .

and then palette-knifed a two-inch frame inside the violet frame. When this was dry, I applied a thin wash of copper paint over it.

After the "frames" were dry, I began building the middle square of the canvas with layers of textured white papers, art tissue, and matte medium. After this had dried, I repeated the process with more layered paper.

After everything was dry, I painted with opaque and transparent acrylics in a spontaneous manner. I loved the glowing effect of the copper symbols that were drawn into the outer frame.

What a joy to texture, layer paint, and embed my personal "journal" into this piece! Would you believe my great grandmother's high-top shoes, which I wore last Halloween, became part of this painting?

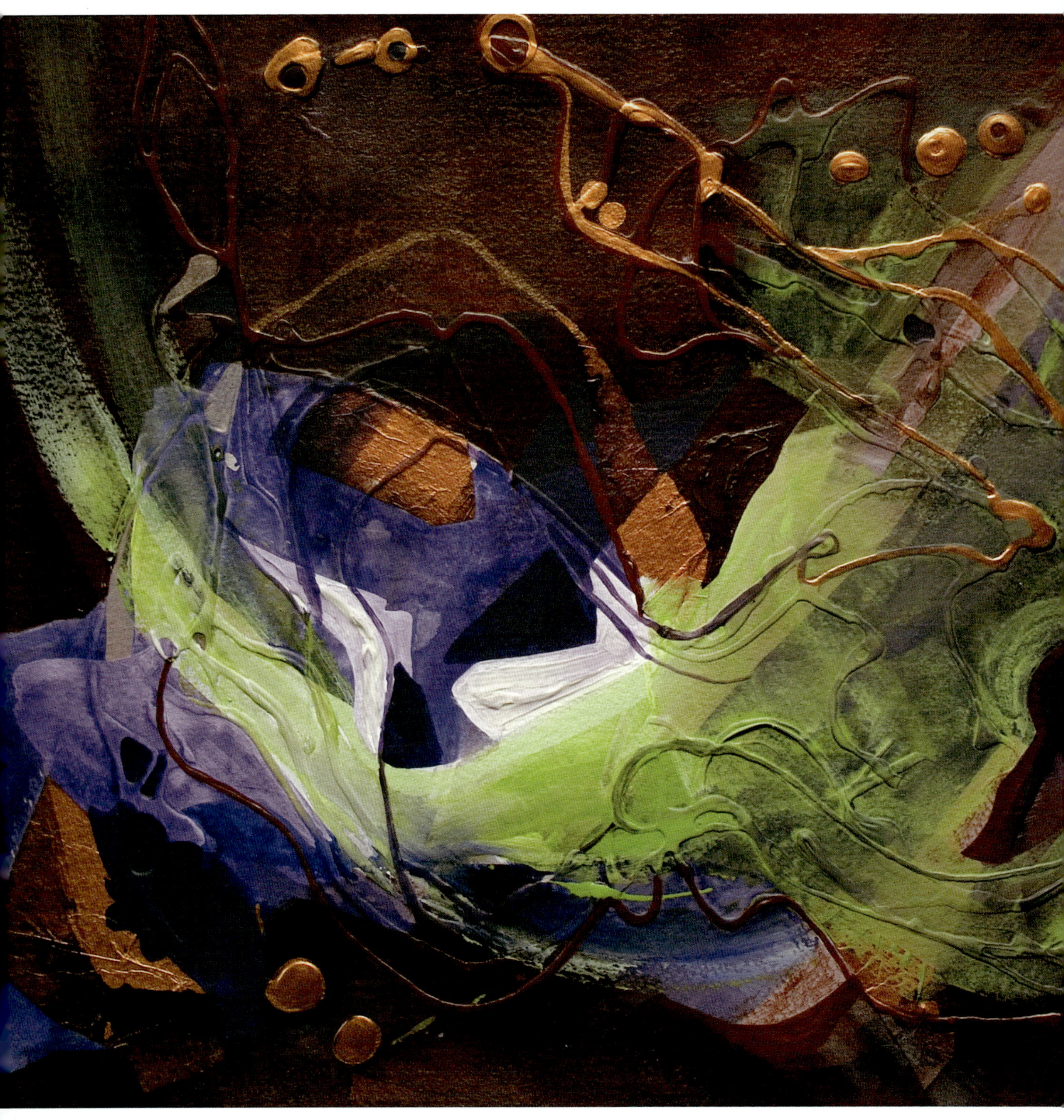

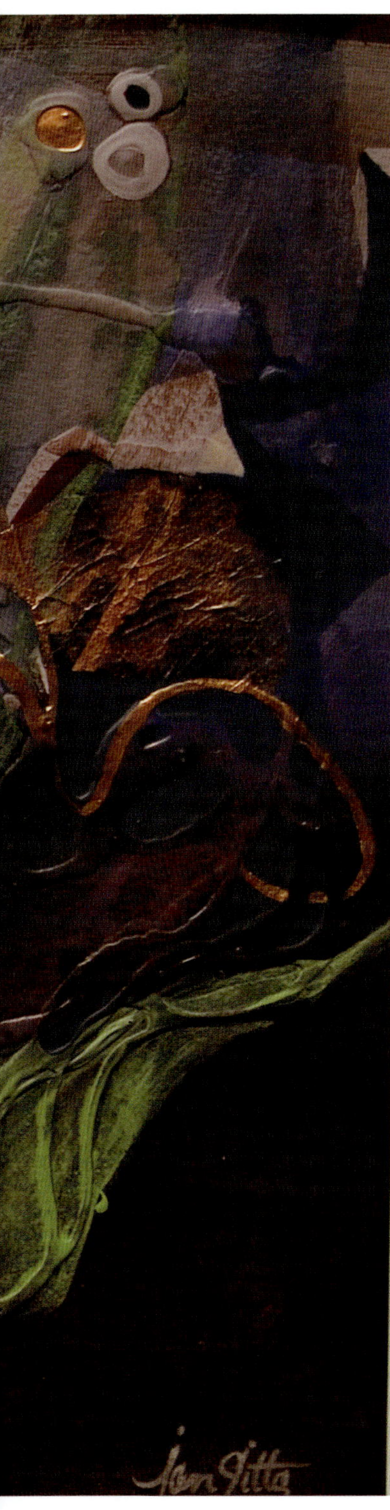

Summary of technique: Gossamer Wings

Gossamer Wings was painted on 300-pound cold press Arches watercolor paper. The background layer of color was painted in alizarin crimson acrylic plus a small bit of black gesso. When these colors combined, a beautiful rich wine color emerged.

After allowing the paint to dry, I applied white gesso in a wide looping swath across the paper, then gave parts of the background a thin wash of lime green paint. I allowed the piece to dry.

I spontaneously drew squiggles and dots across the piece using Elmer's Glue. The glue took about twenty-four hours to dry.

I carefully painted over the raised glue surfaces with a Number 6 round acrylic brush to give the effect of a relief using copper metallic paint. The copper applied over the squiggles created a heavy, thick line against the gauzy lime green wash. I applied other colors to areas of the painting.

After turning the piece in all directions, I realized it needed two more long, uneven glue lines to break up a large negative space and unify the composition. So I repeated the process above with glue and metallic paint.

The contrast in this piece never ceases to amaze me! The dark colors contrast with the light colors, and the filmy washes look like floating gauze. It was the final "aha" to this spontaneous painting.

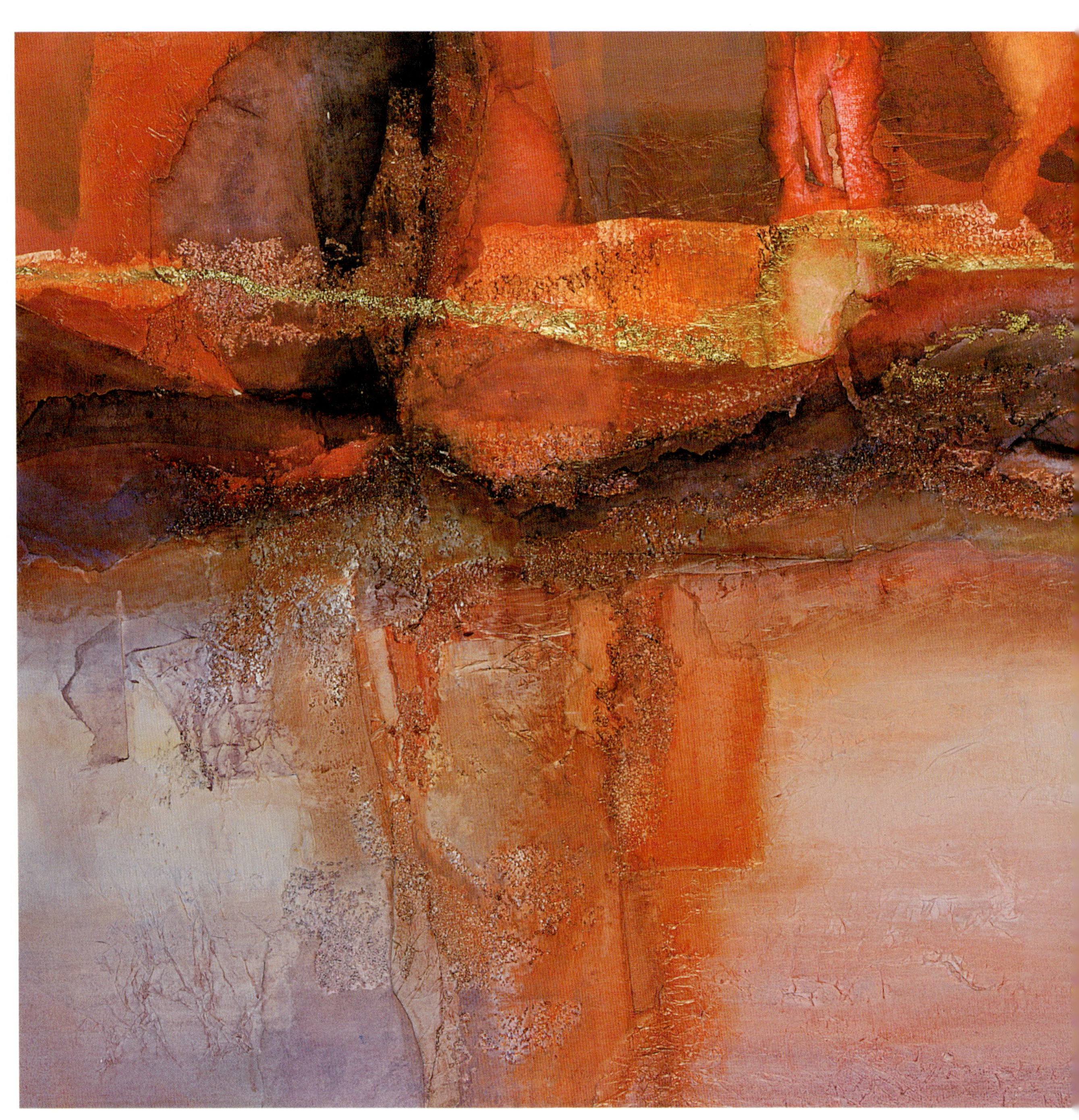

Summary of technique: Summer Solstice

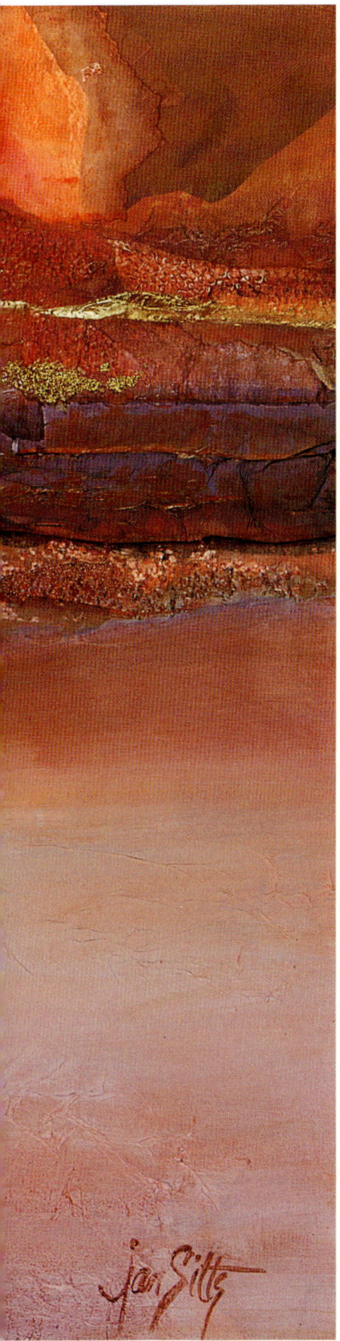

The horizon line of this painting was drawn in with pencil on the pre-gessoed canvas.

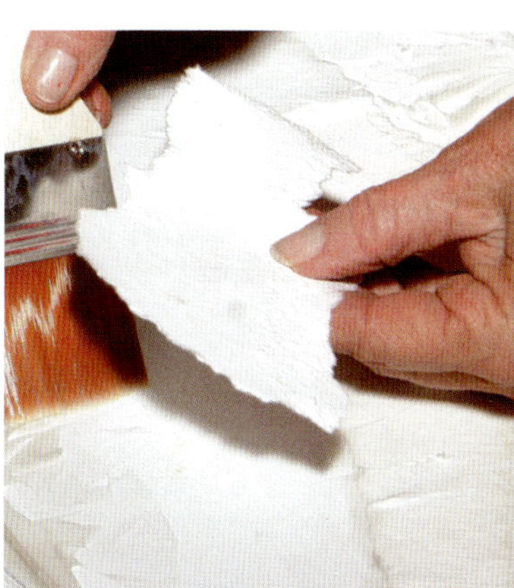

100% cotton rag paper shapes were cut and torn and applied to the canvas with acrylic matte medium.

When the previous steps were completed and the piece was dry, I took a large palette knife and spread glass bead textured gel over areas of the canvas to give the look of stratification for the "rock" areas.

After the layered textures were dry, I painted the surface of the piece in my normal fashion using warm hues.

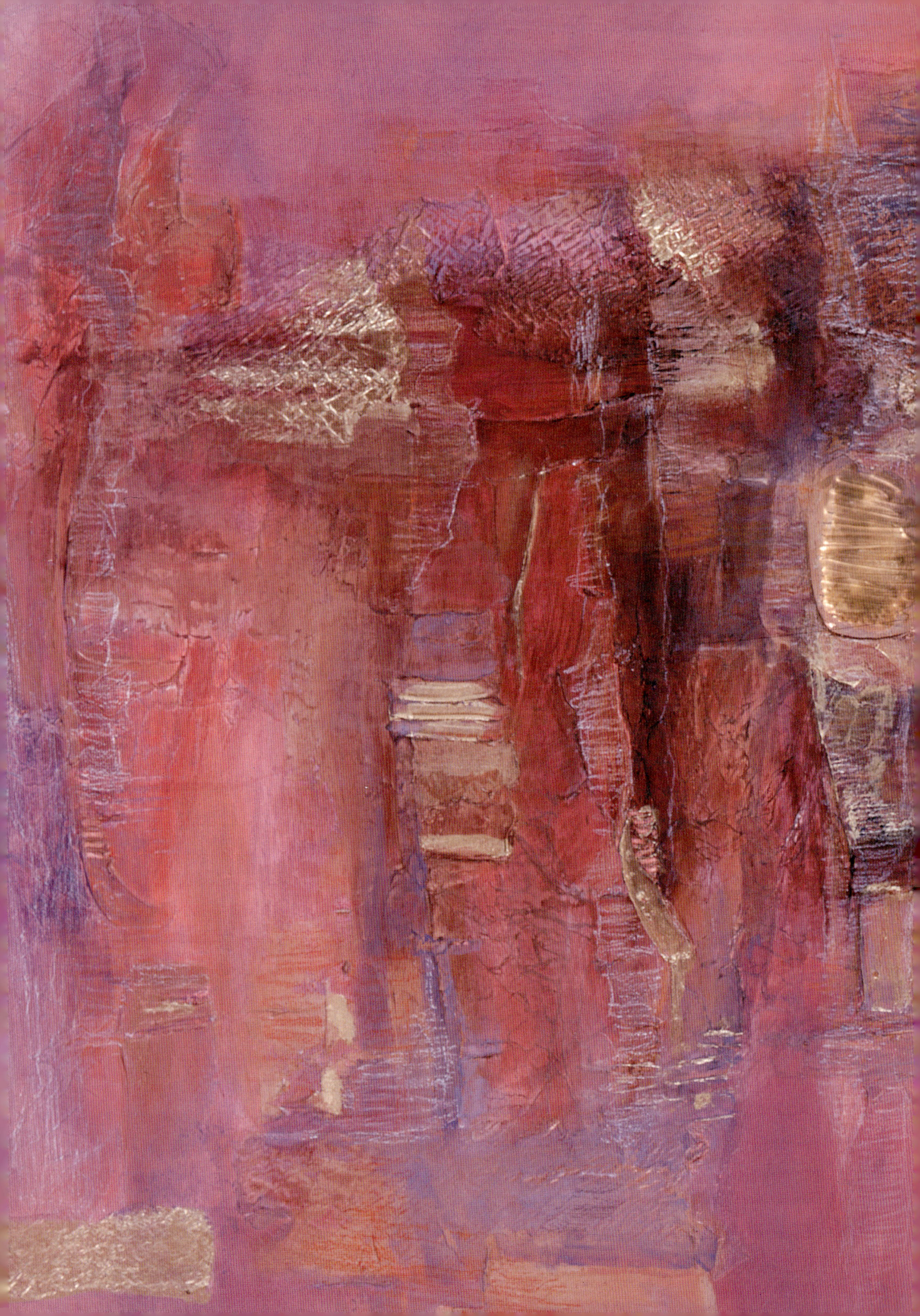

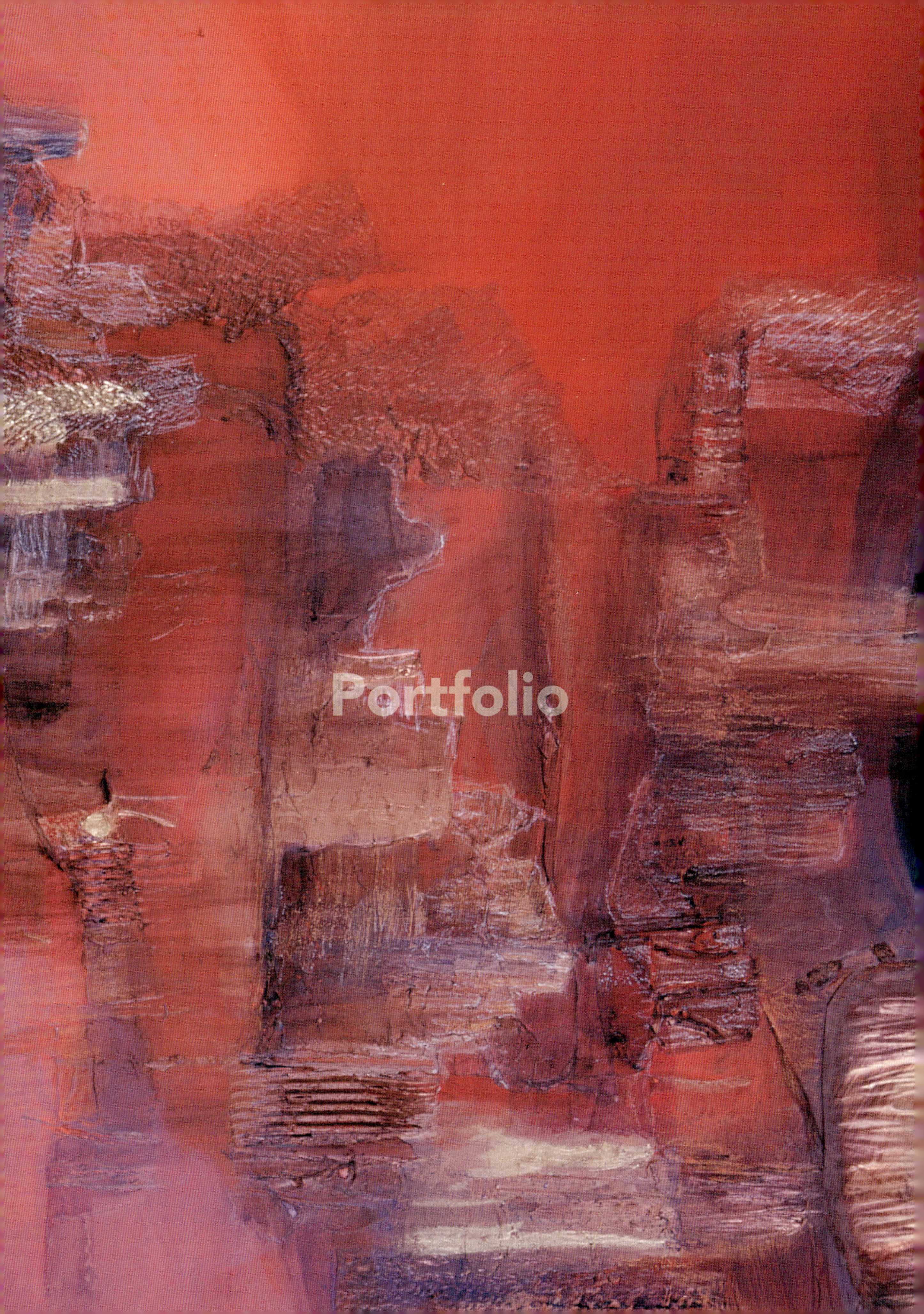
Portfolio

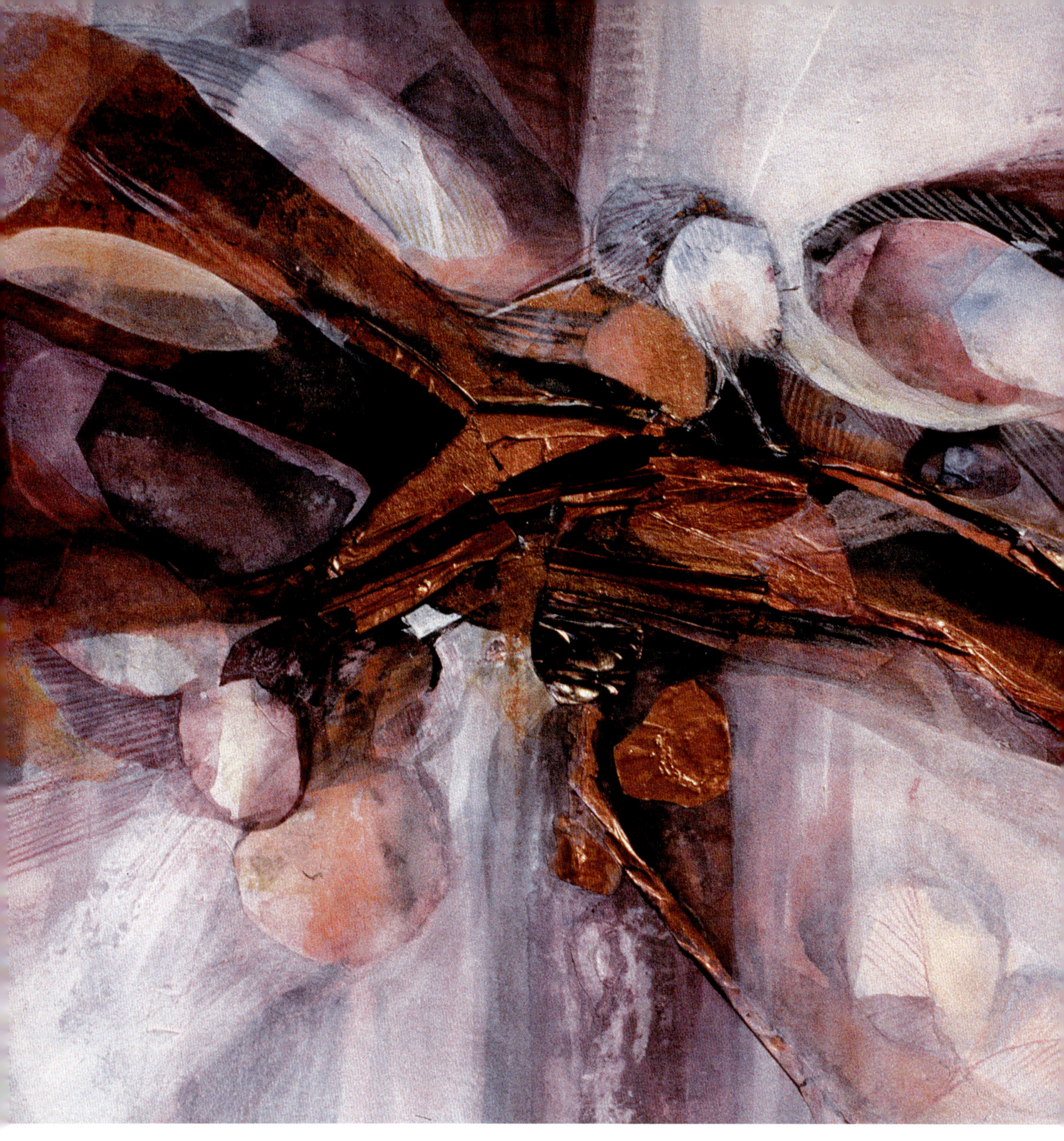

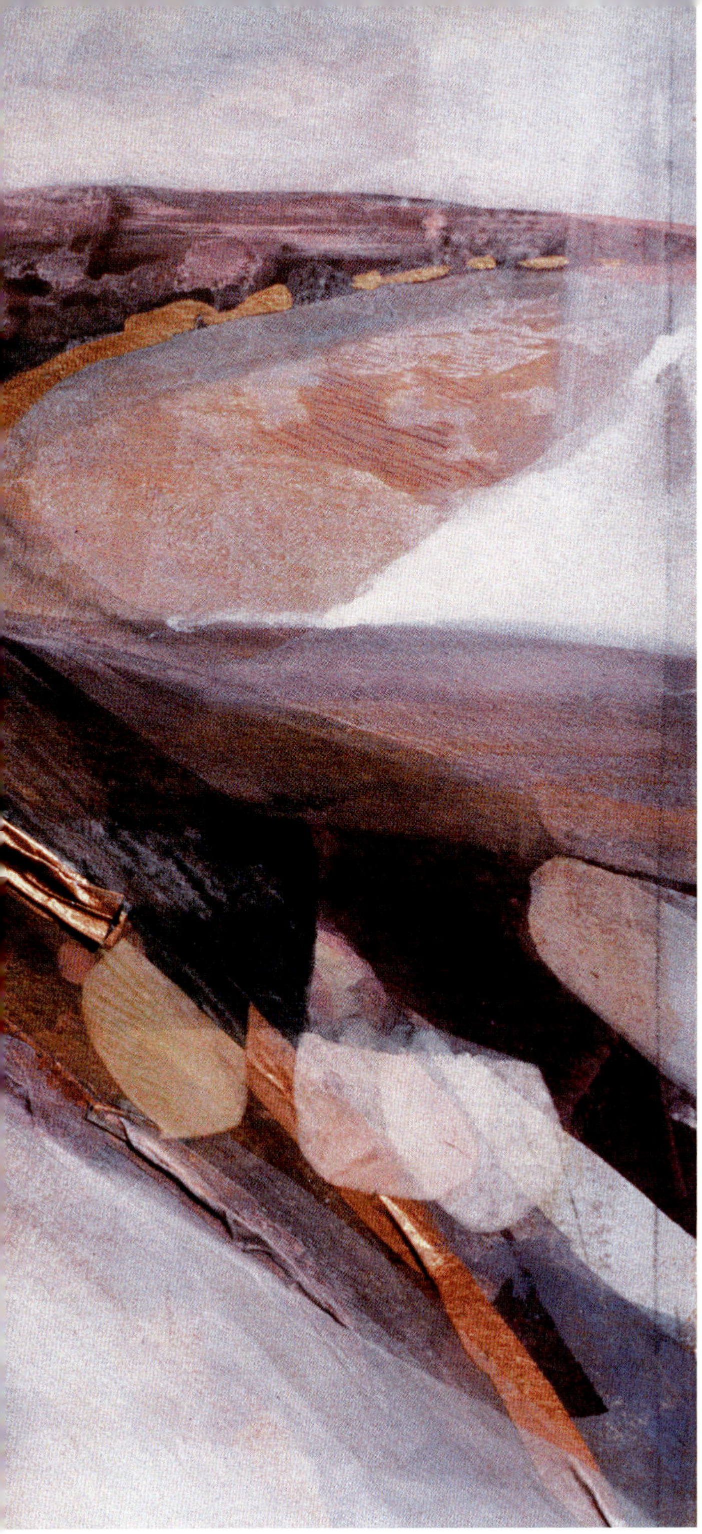

Using art tissue paper in my work is always a fun experience. The unusual textures it provides always seems to make the piece come alive. I painted the tissue with copper paint. After it dried, I rolled it into tube-like forms. These created the branches for the nest. After designing the rest of the painting and completing the bird shapes, I hatched with white pencils over the dark washes to define the forms.

NESTING

22 x 30, mixed media on canvas

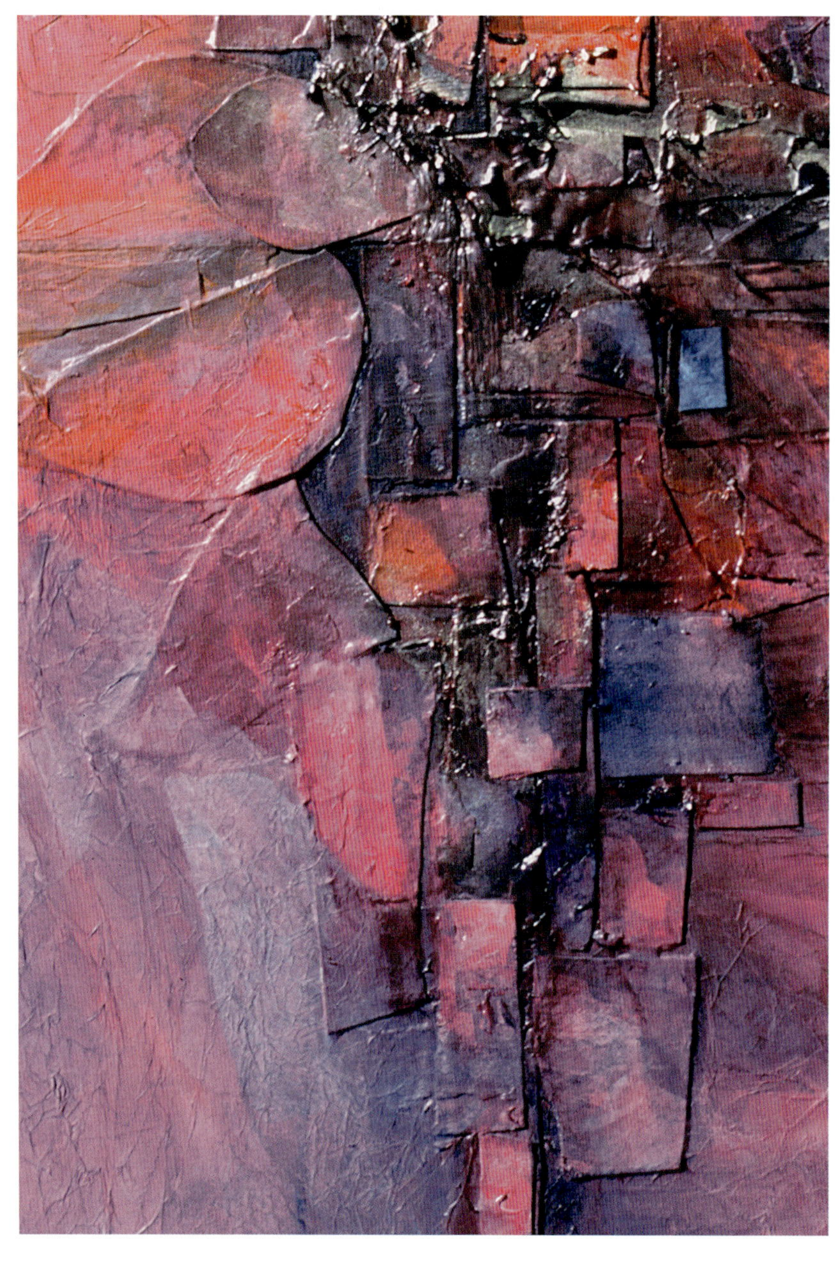

NURTURING THE SOUL 36 x 48, mixed media on canvas

GREENSWARD (DETAIL)

24 x 36, mixed media on canvas

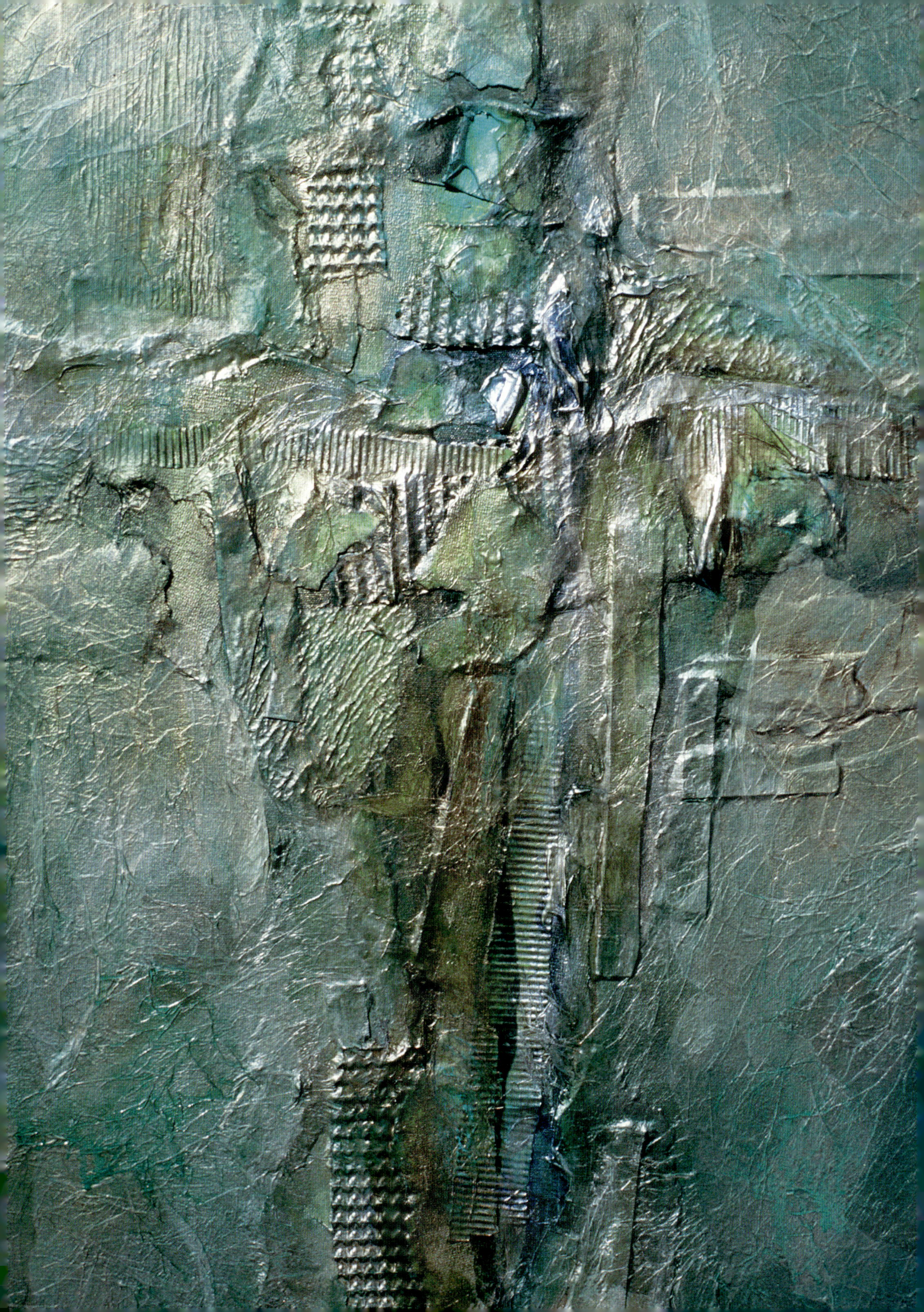

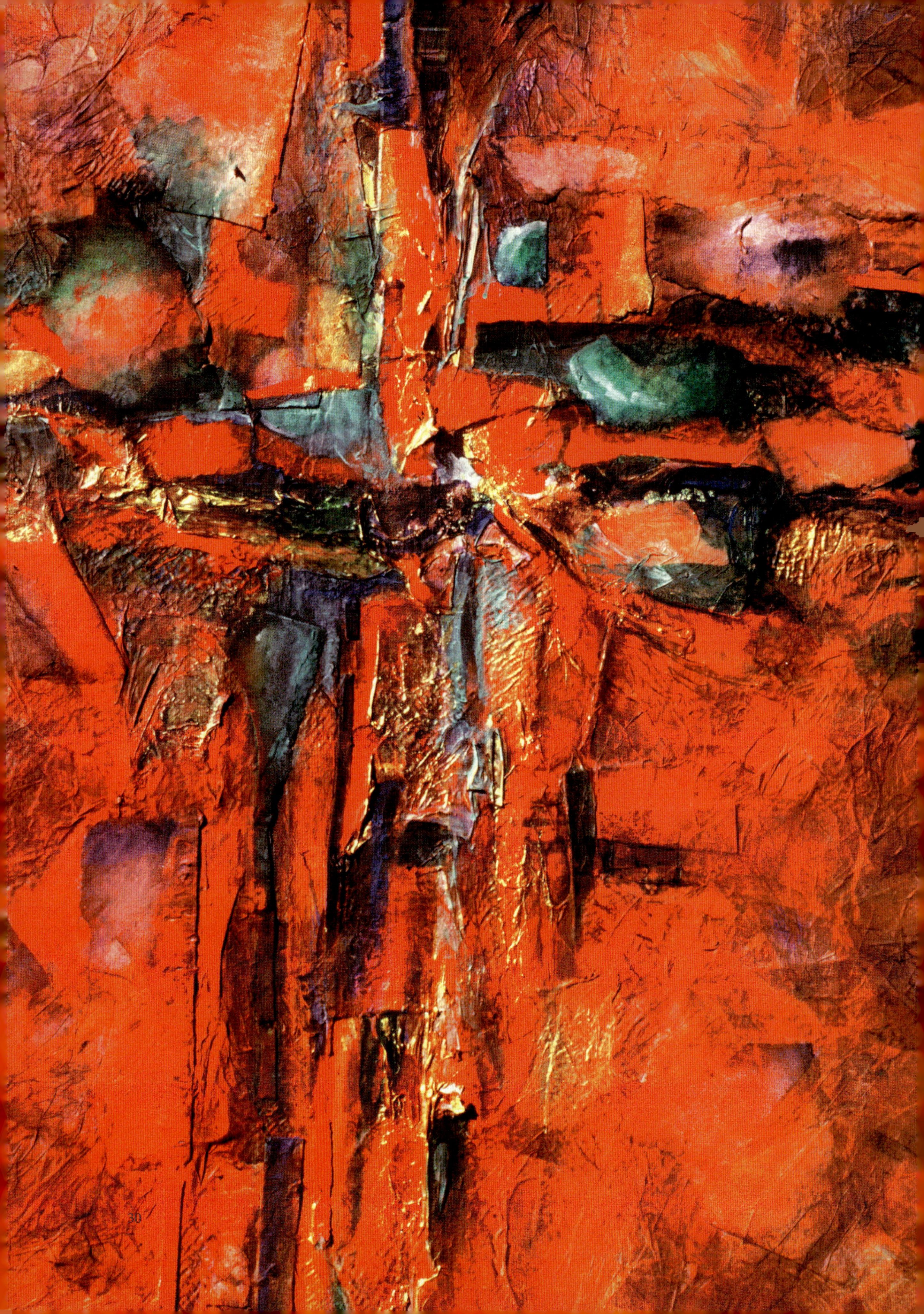

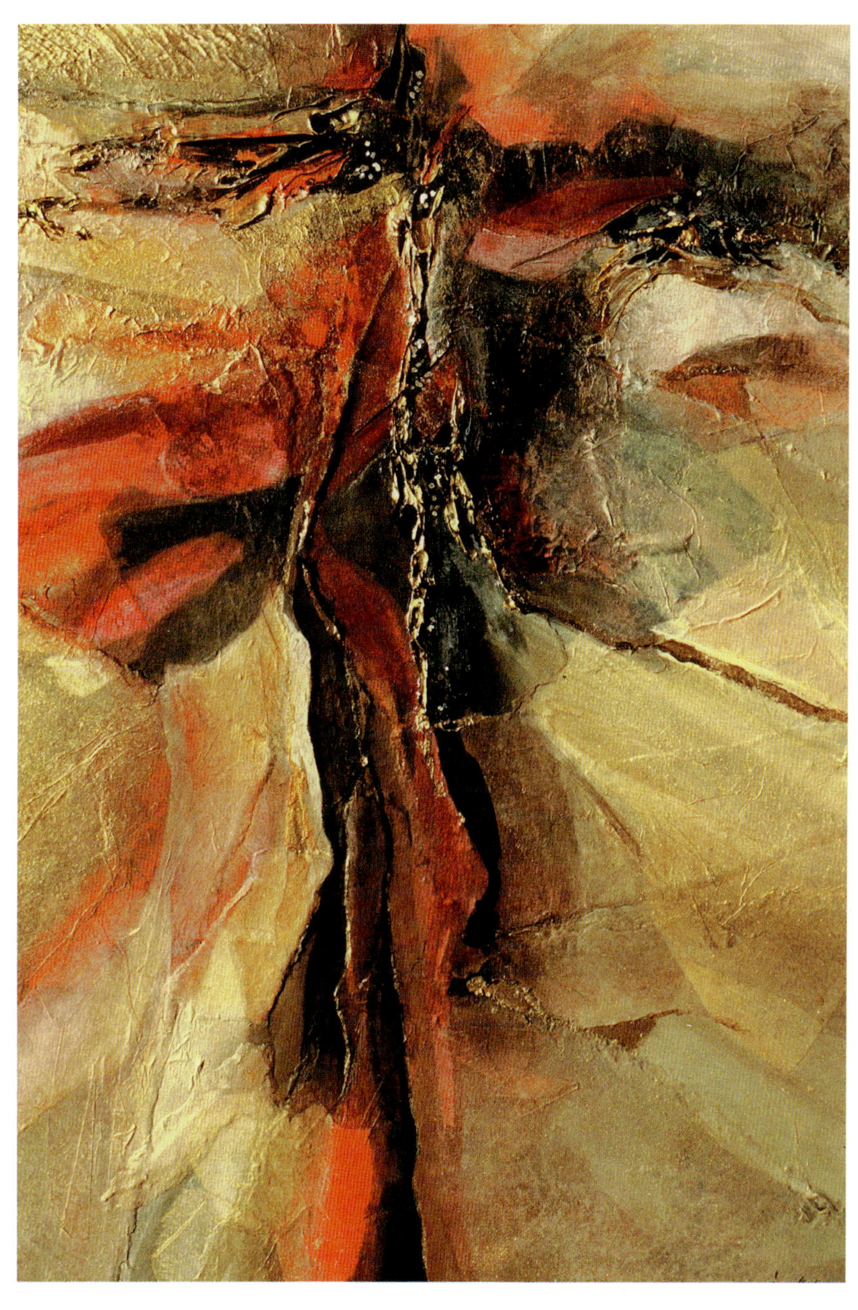

THE PAINTED LADY 30 x 36, mixed media on canvas

WINTERGREEN DECEMBER (DETAIL)

36 x 48, mixed media on canvas

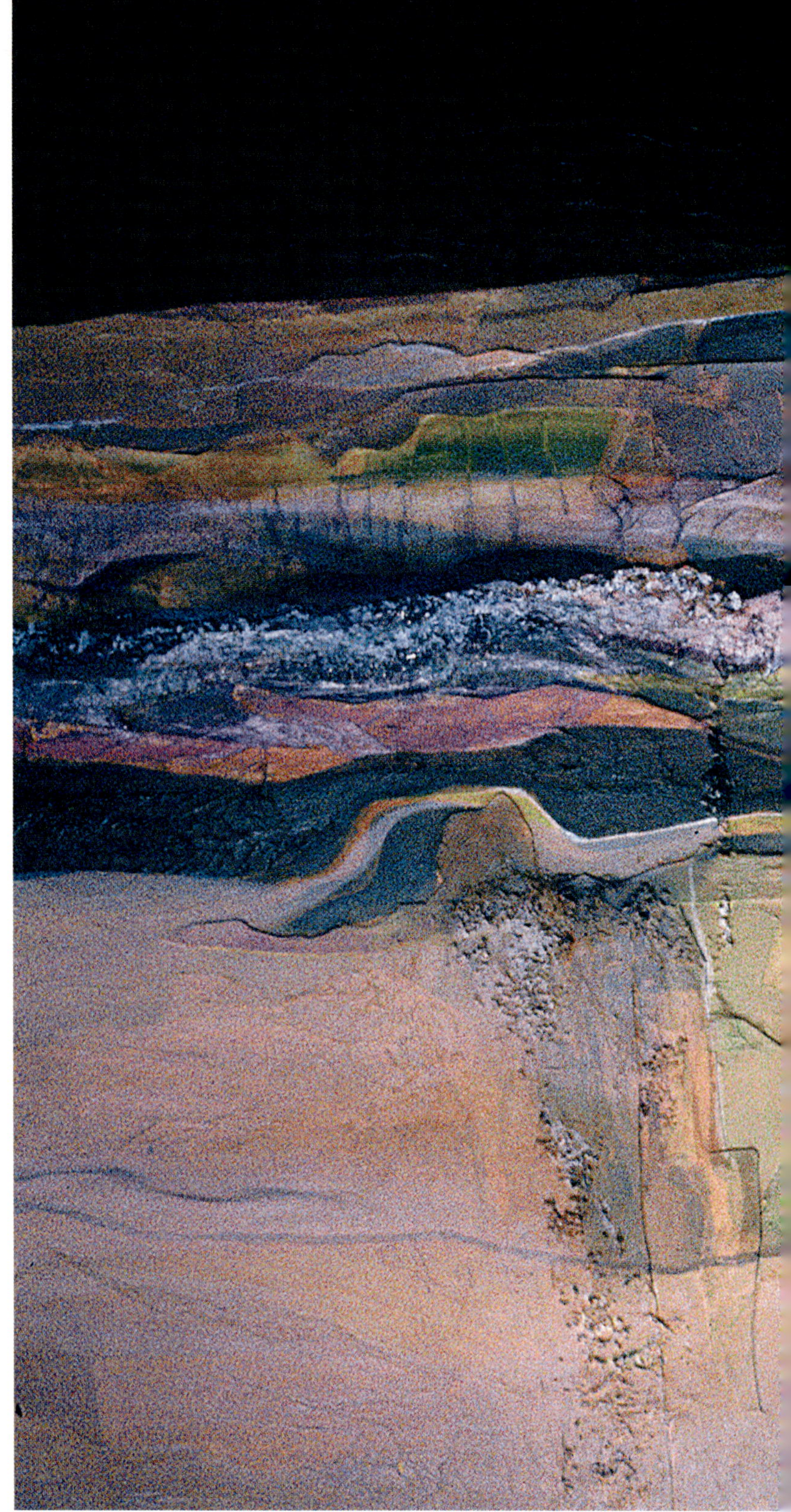

JEWELS PEAK

36 x 48, mixed media on canvas

This is a very special landscape in opaque and a variety of arbitrary color. It is in the collection of Jim and Dorothy Valcarsel of Sedona, Arizona.

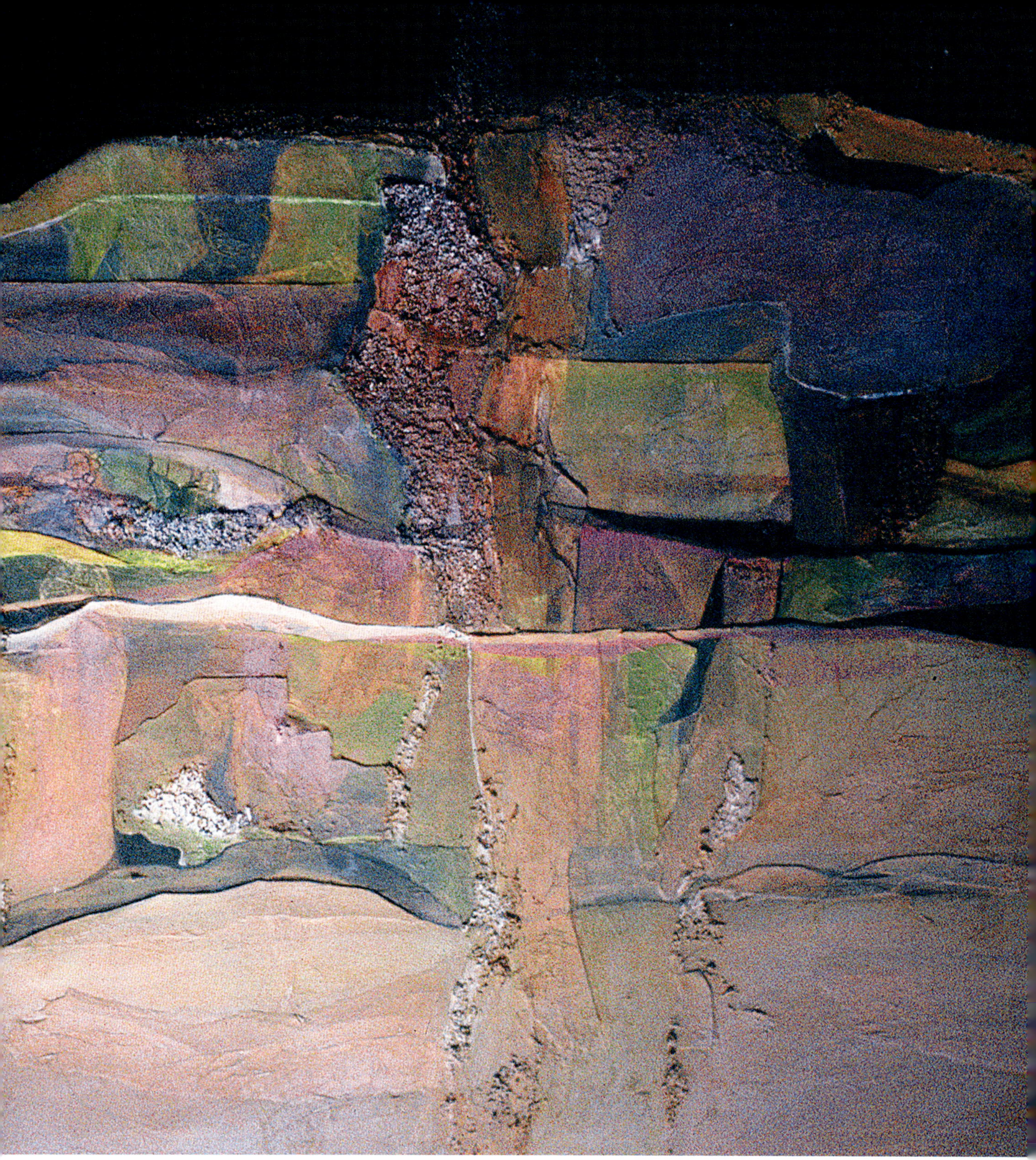

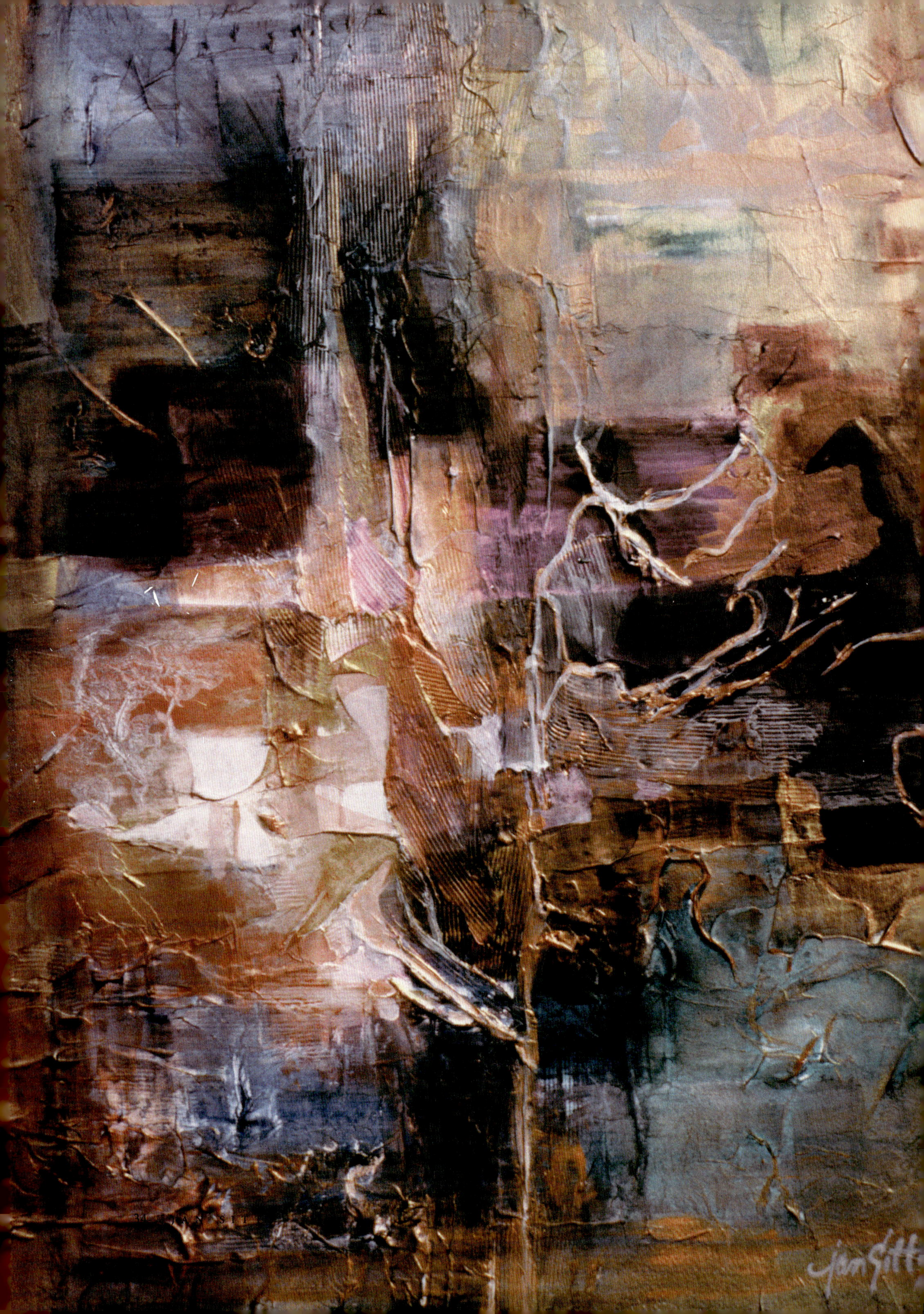

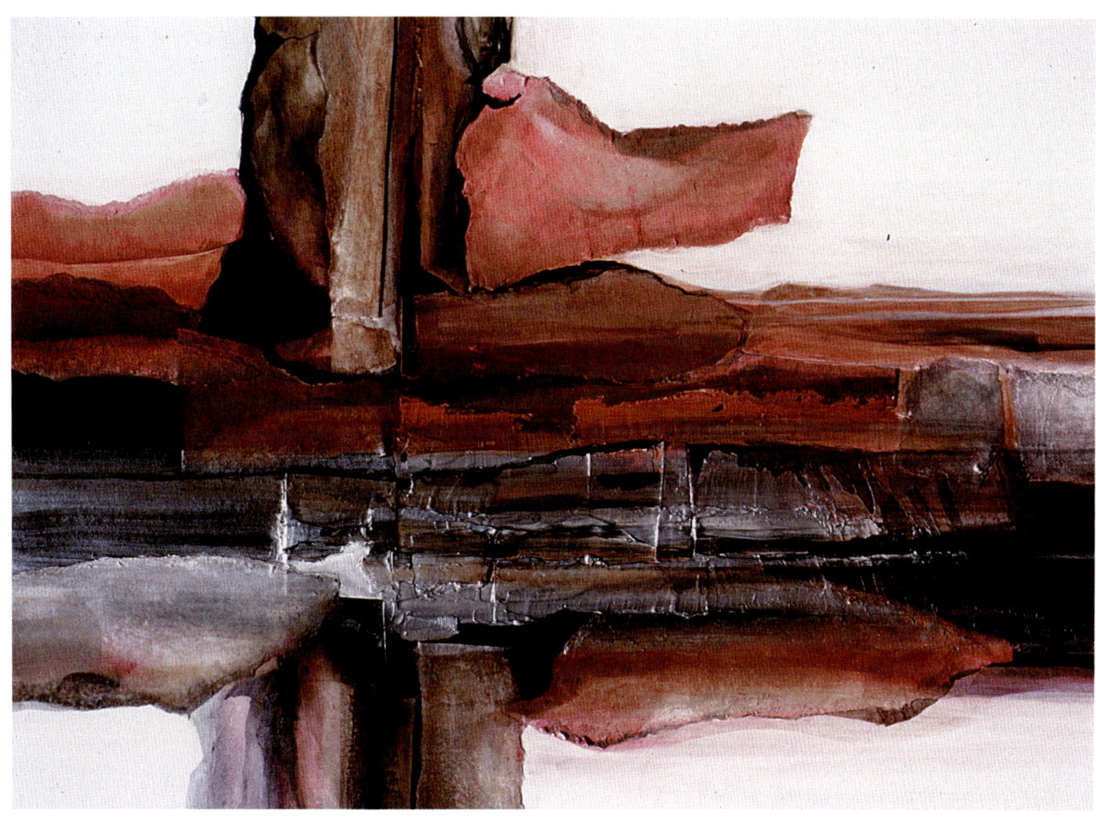

SPIRIT OF SEDONA

36 x 48, mixed media on canvas

Spirit of Sedona was painted in 2001 and is in the collection of Peter and Janet Fagan of Sedona, Arizona. A Southwest feeling of longhorns and rawhide.

LOST LAKE (DETAIL)

22 x 30, mixed media on watercolor paper

I was grateful to spend summers with my cousins on their farm. This painting is filled with memories of the pond nearby. I loved the old rope swing that took us out over the mysterious waters where we held our noses and made our big jump. There was never a moment that I wasn't scared, but the lure of the natural surroundings calmed my spirit.

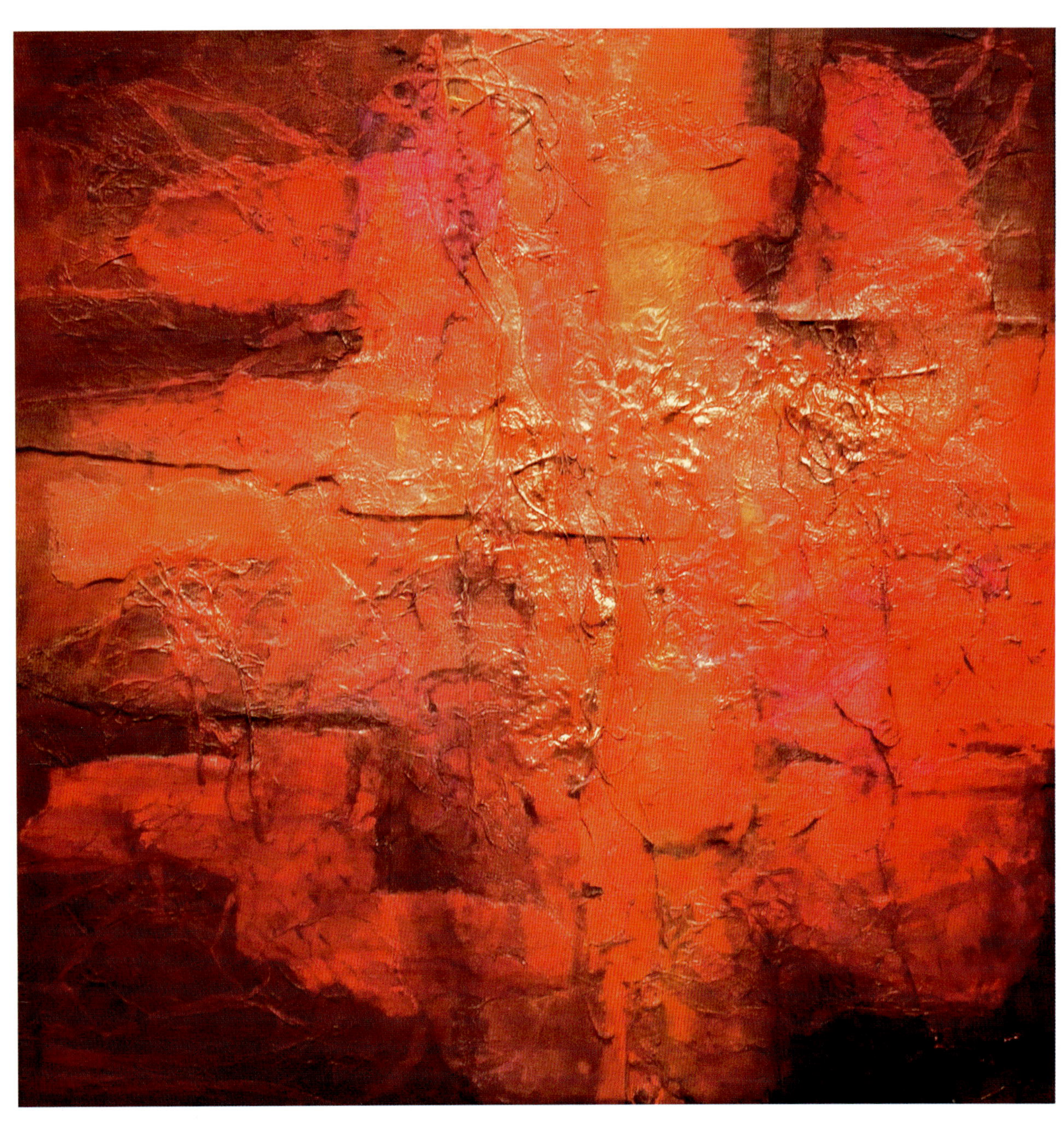

ARDENT FIRES 18 x 18, mixed media on canvas

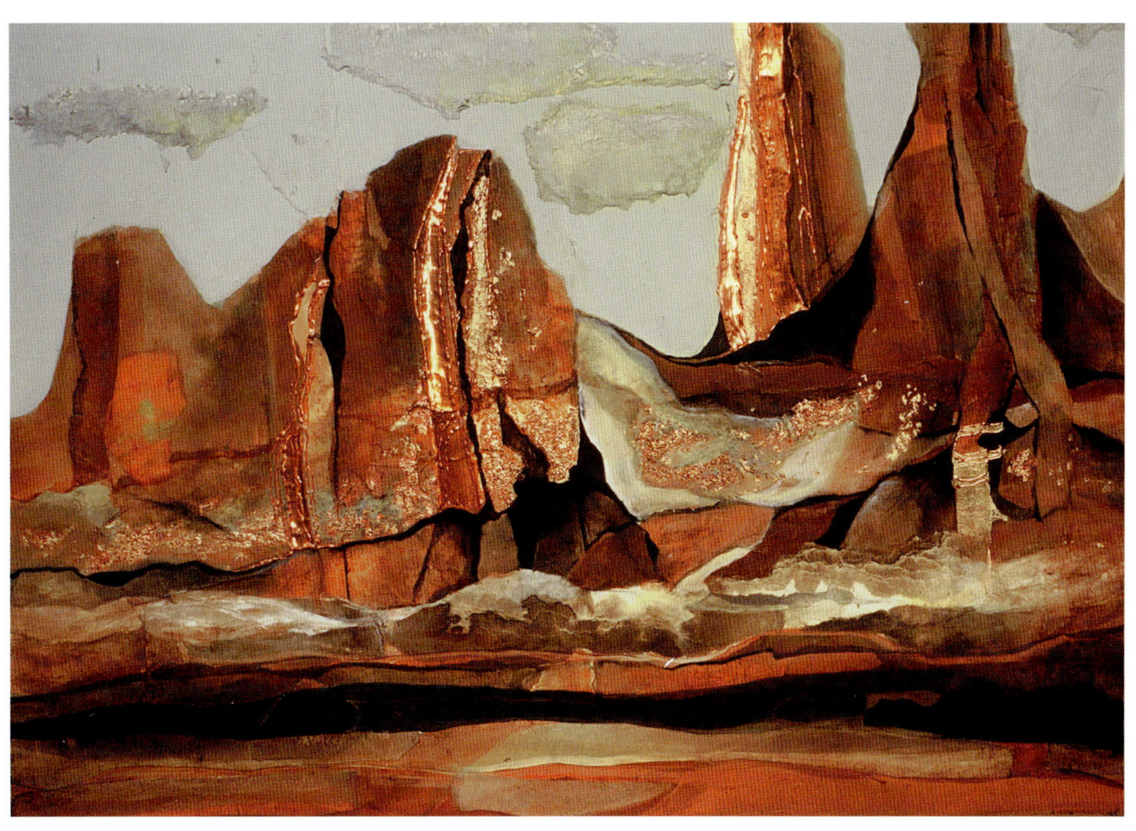

SEDONA IN COPPER 36 x 48, mixed media on canvas

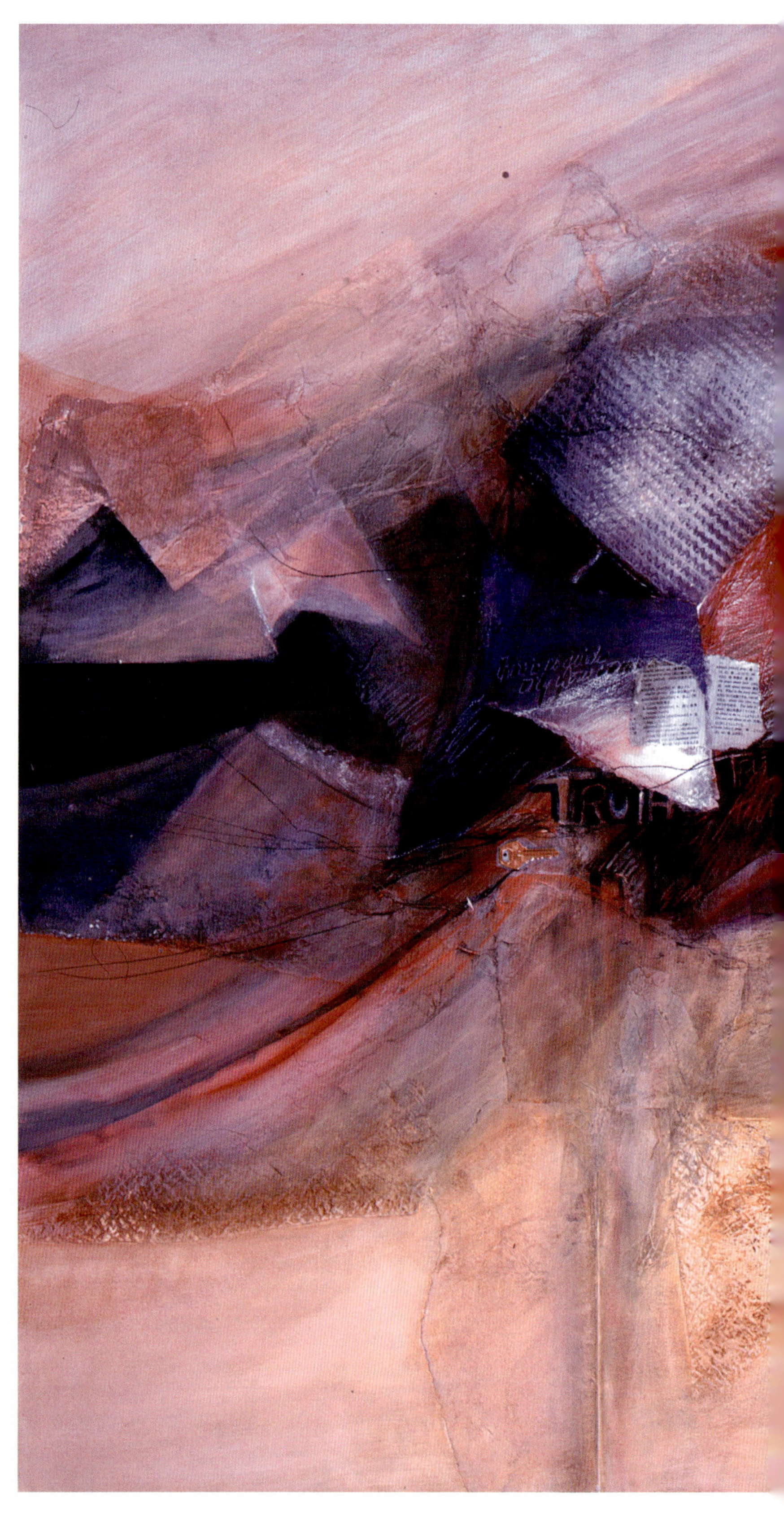

LETTERS OF TRUTH

36 x 48, mixed media on canvas

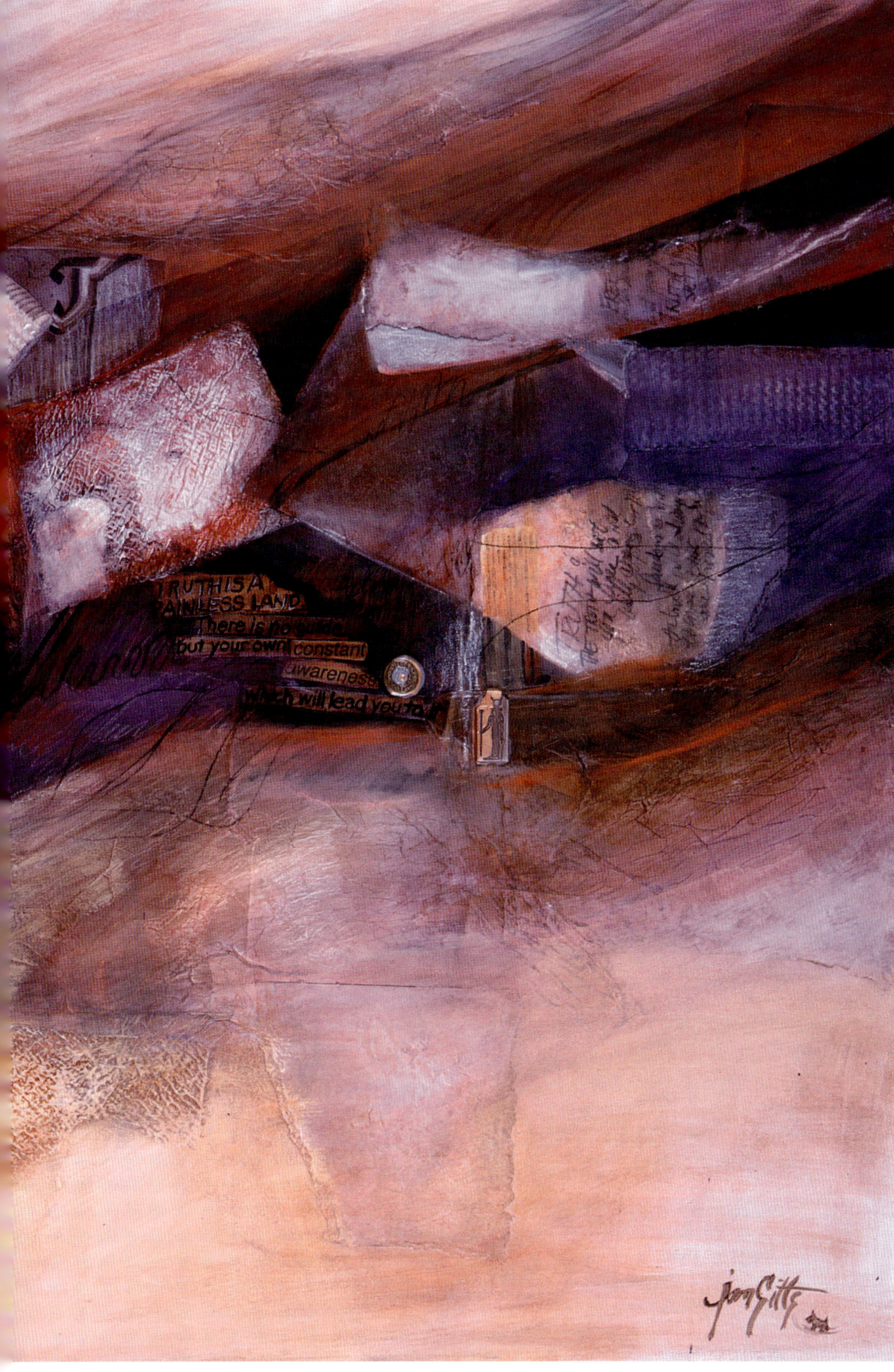
TRUTH IS A
There is no
but your own constant
awareness
will lead you

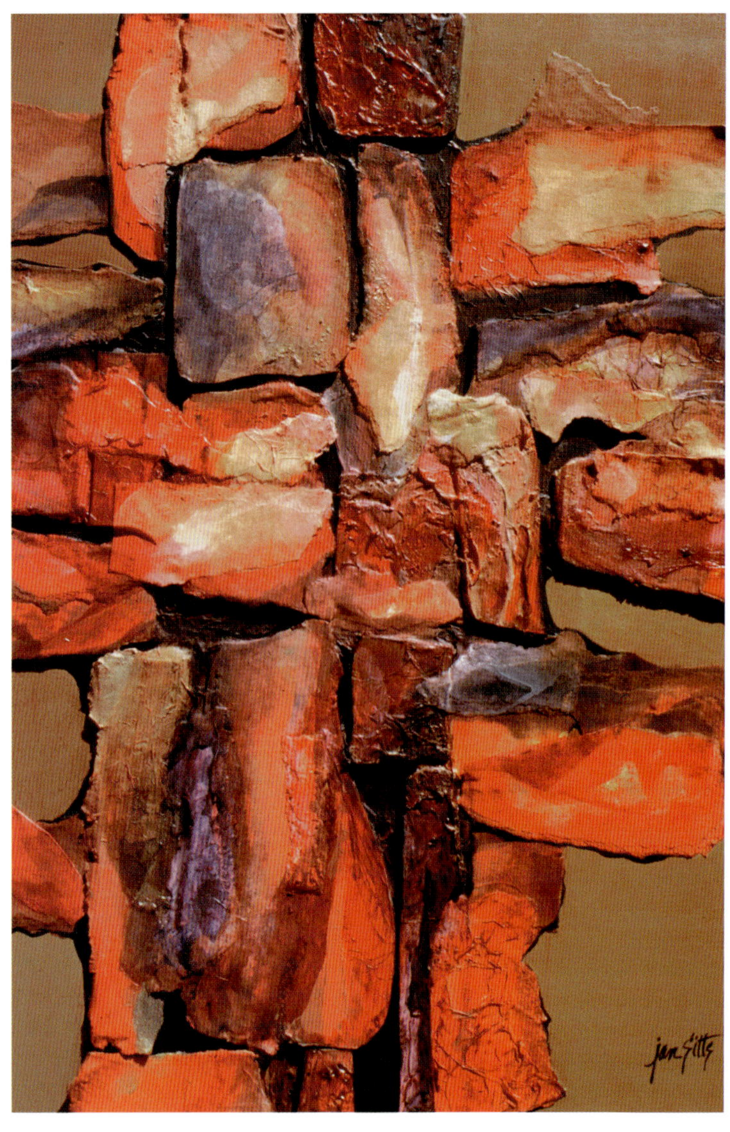

SEDONA

22 x 30, mixed media on canvas

I was commissioned to do a piece for the Sedona Sculpture Walk in 2002. An art collector from Phoenix saw the resulting painting in a magazine ad and phoned me to purchase the piece. I told him that if he really wanted the piece he would have to call in his bid around noon on the day of the auction or be present at the Sculpture Walk in Sedona. Failing to do either, with minutes ticking away, he called the Sedona Police Department and described the painting, and officers drove out to the Sculpture Walk auction and retrieved it for him with their bid. A good deed turned out great for all!

FIRE SPIRIT (DETAIL) 22 x 30, mixed media on canvas

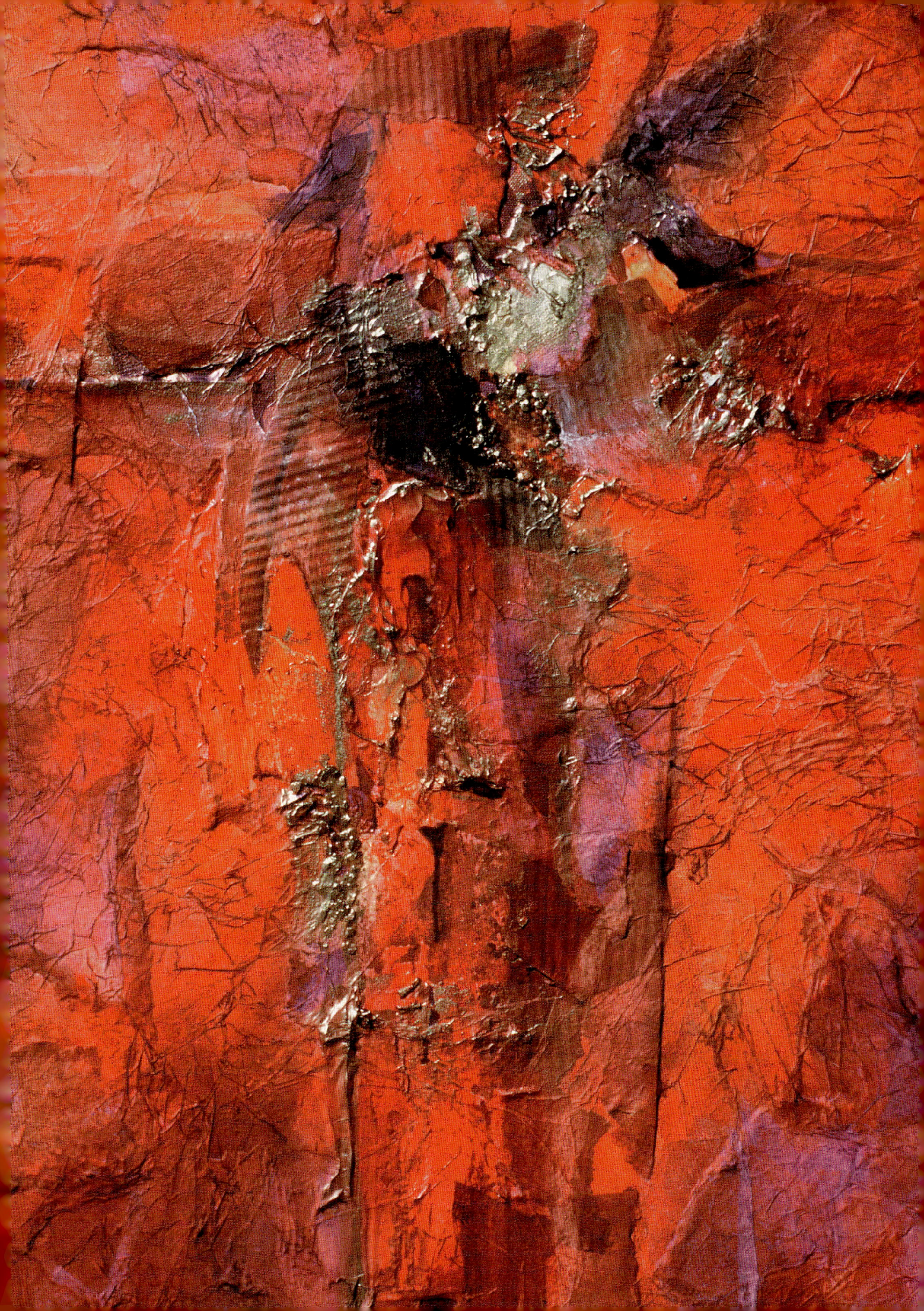

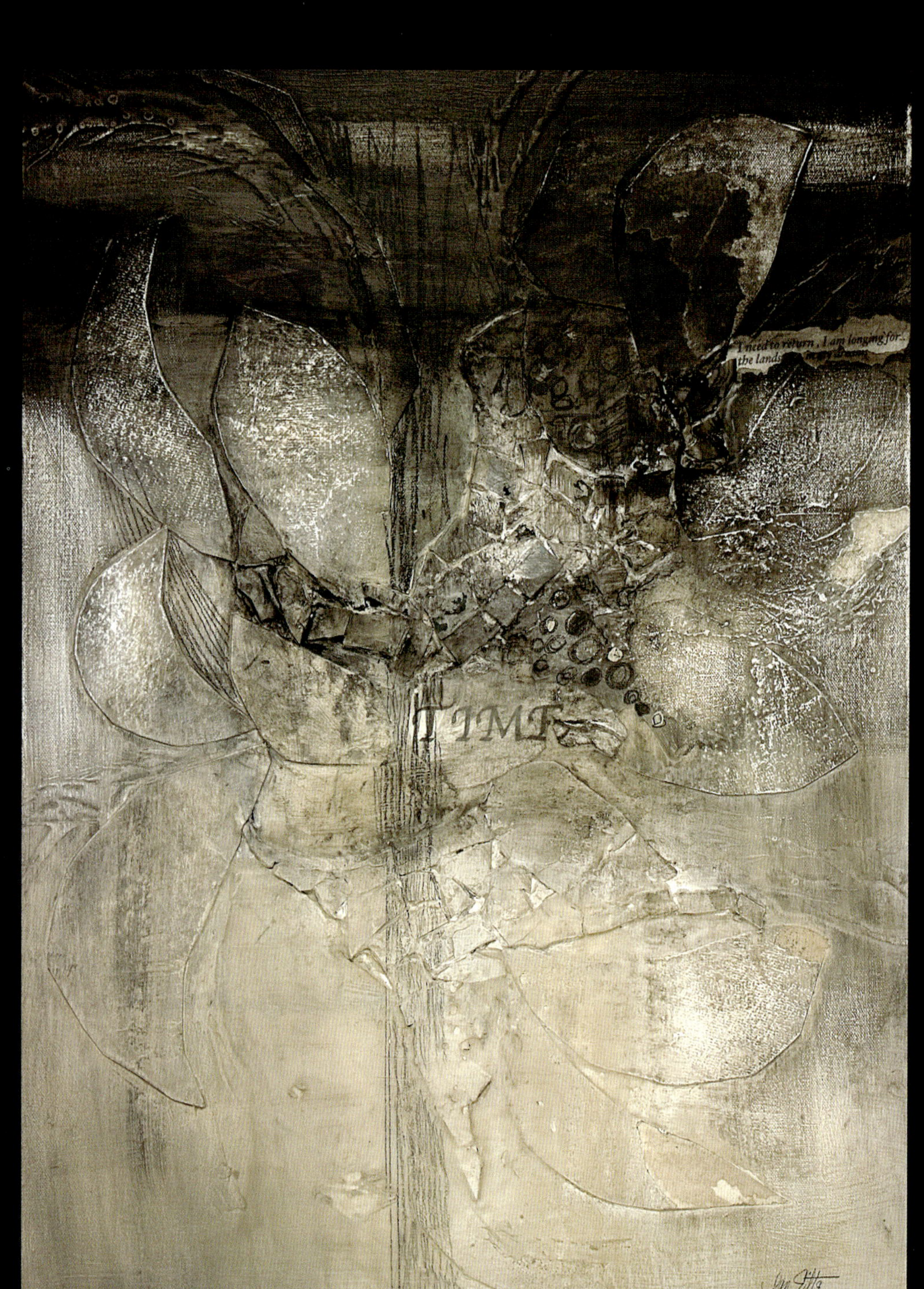
I need to return, I am longing for
the lands
TIME

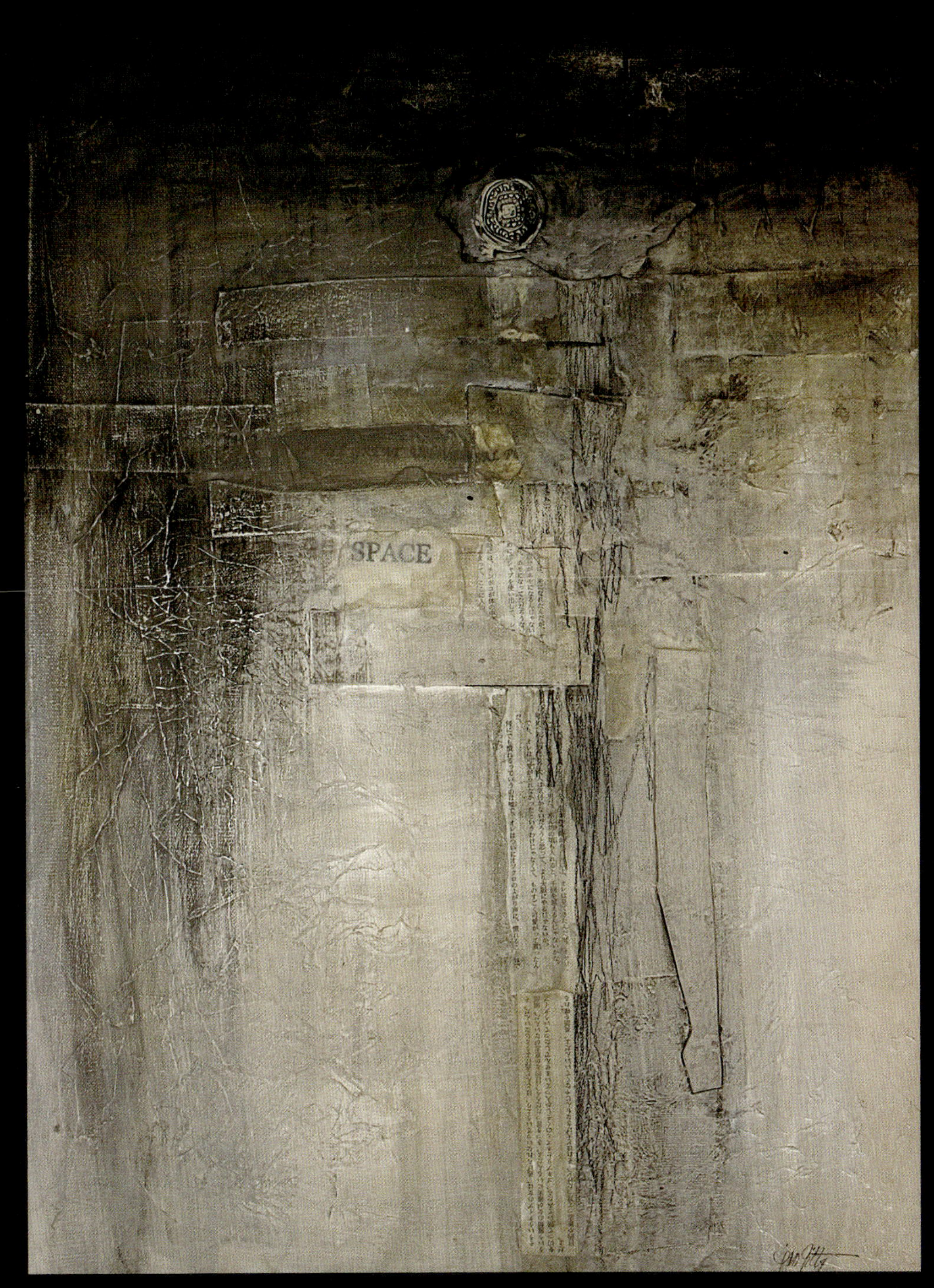
SPACE

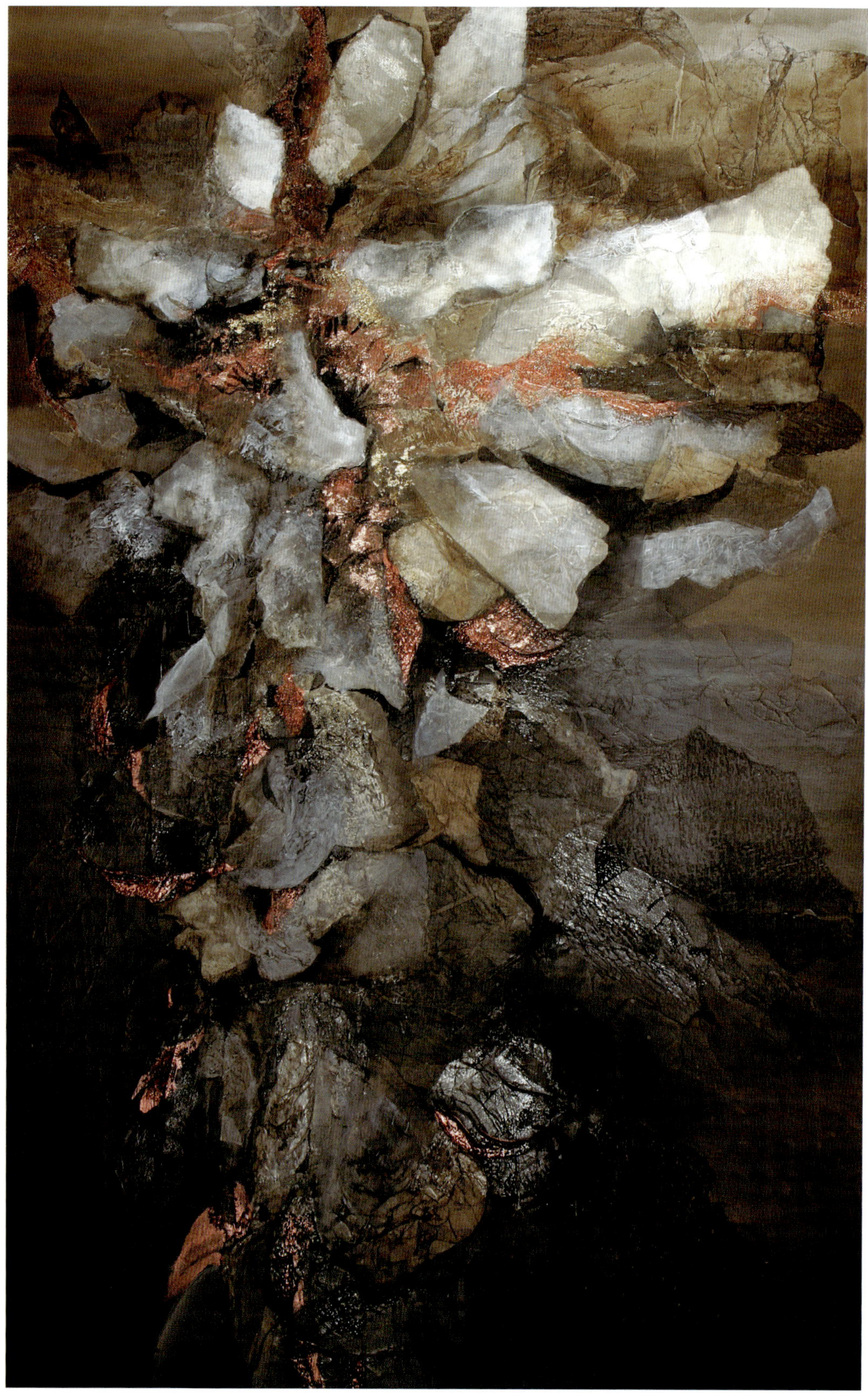

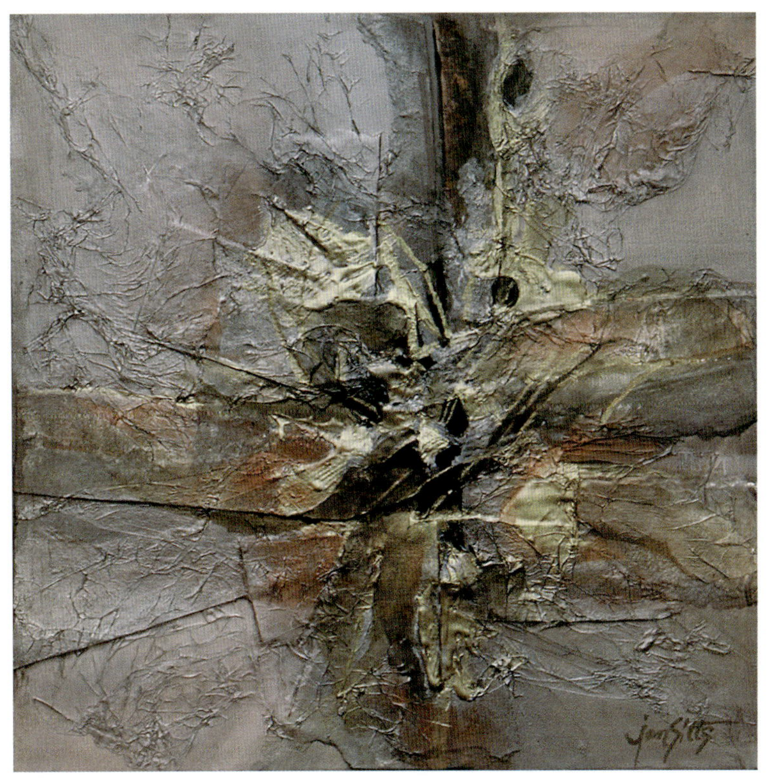

GRAY ORCHID 18 x 18, mixed media on canvas

PAST GLORIES

36 x 60, mixed media on canvas

The fluid petal-like forms and graceful layered shapes take the center stage in this piece. The shadows and light were balanced by choosing a monochromatic palette of warm earth tones. This painting was a spontaneous work developed in quiet celebration, evolving from one of those sacred moments in life. It is in the collection of William J. and Mary M. Platzer of Sedona, Arizona, and Puerto Vallarta, Mexico.

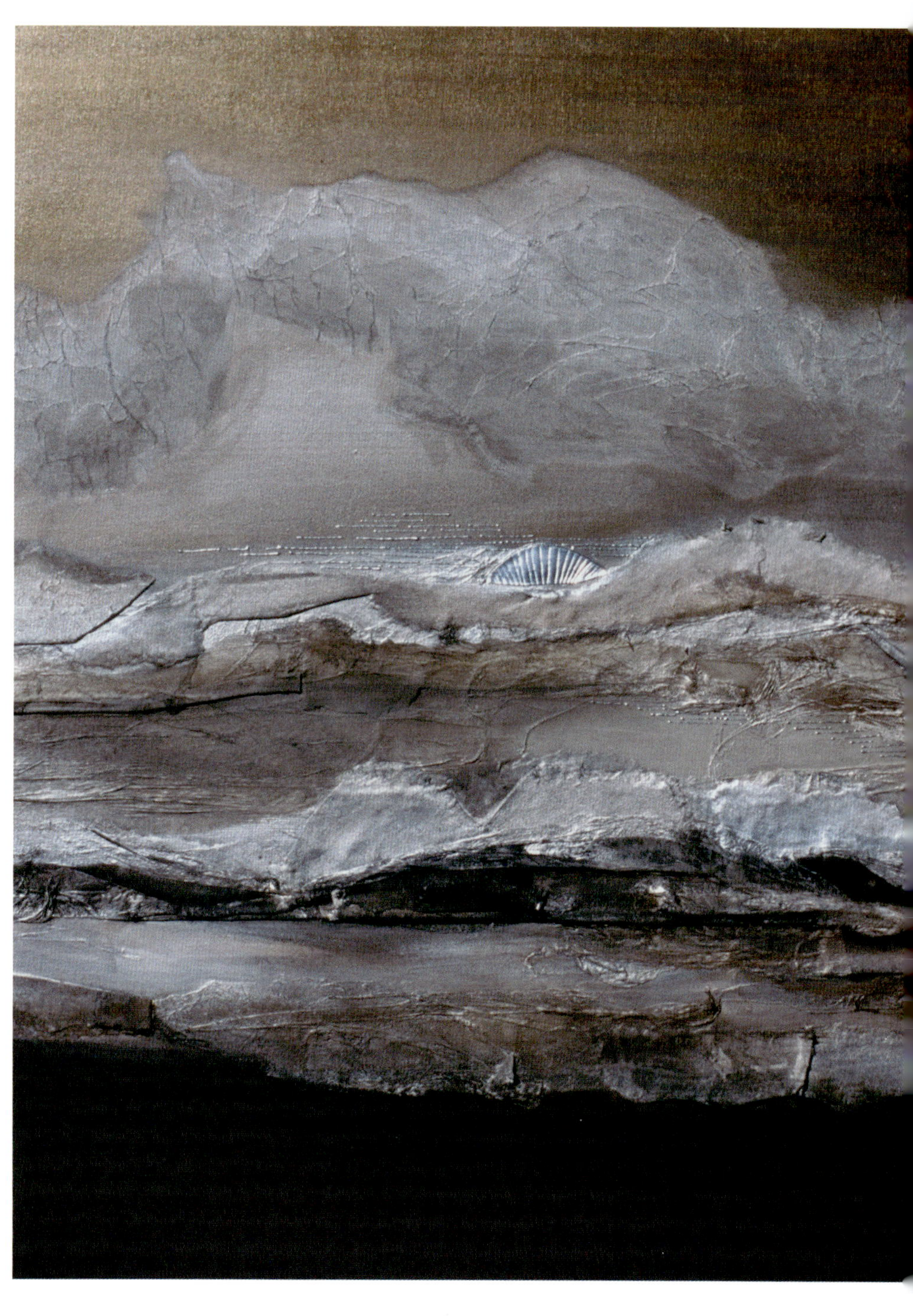

MORNING MIST 36 x 60 mixed media on canvas

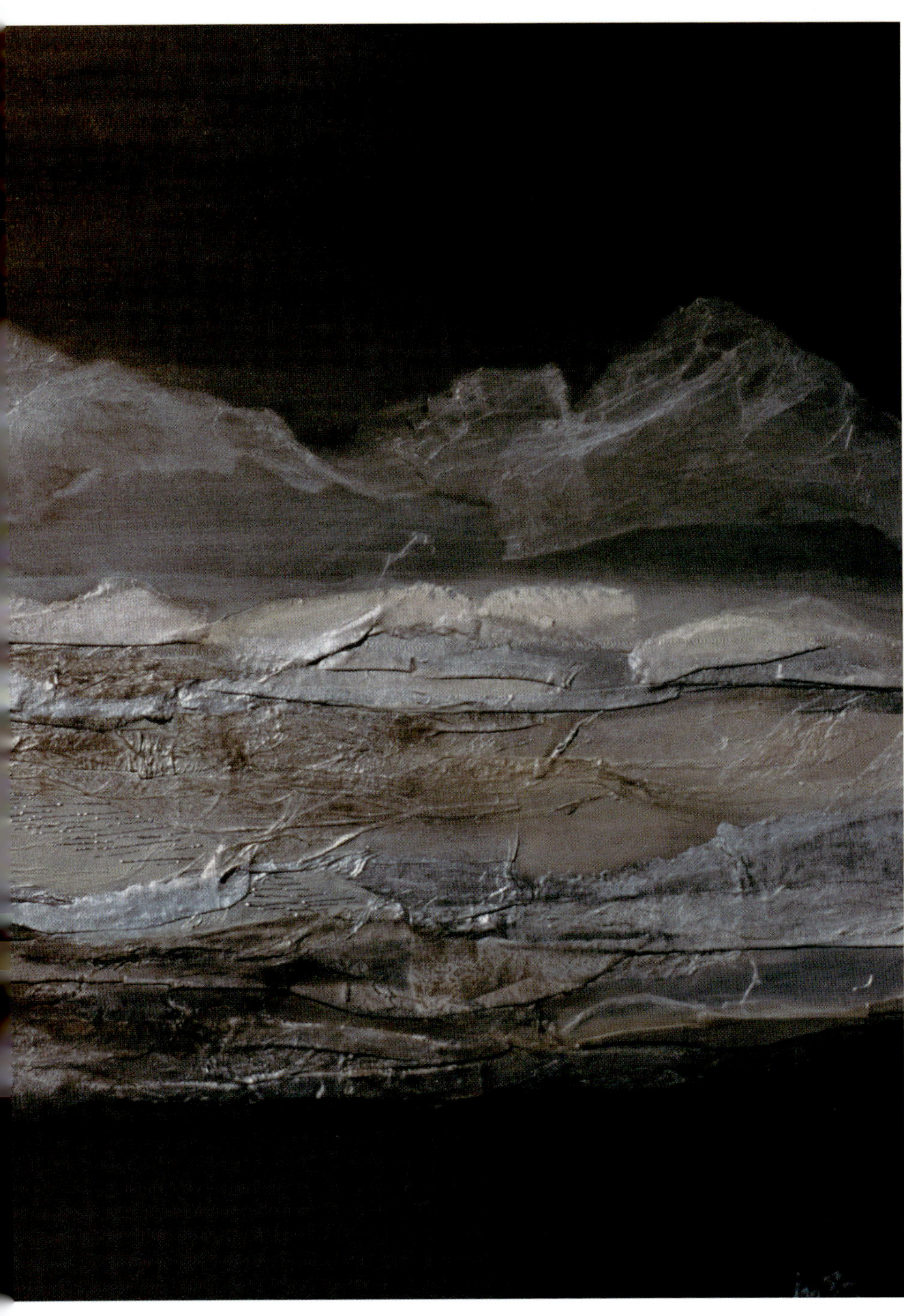

As I began developing this piece with textures I was delighted to see shapes taking the form of ocean waves washing against the shoreline. I used deeper taupe colors under the waves for shadows and a light silver on the wave tops. The soft clouds were developed with tissue and painted transparent white. The sky was painted in low-key bronze and the beach in the deepest taupe color. The sunrise on the horizon was cut out of silver metal.

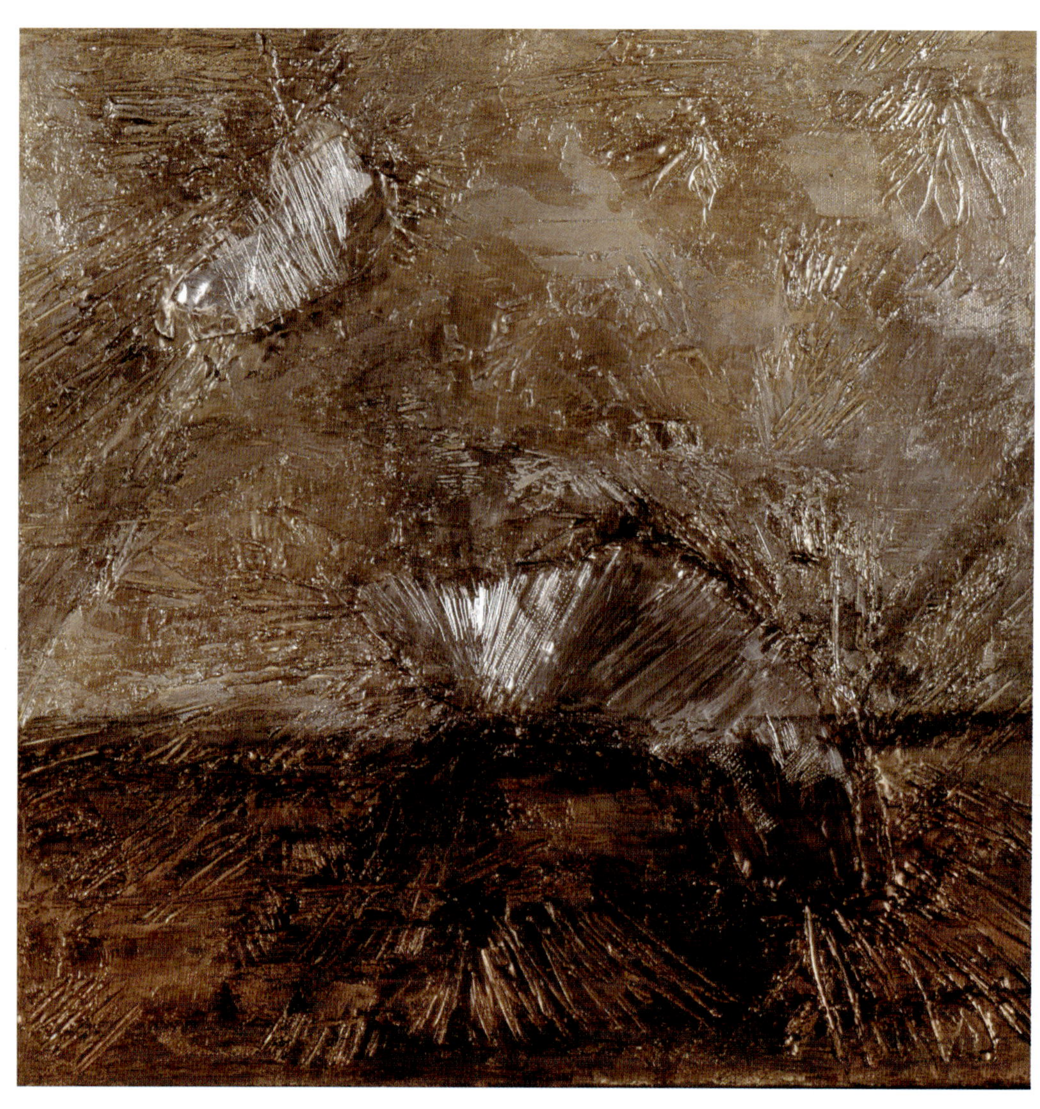

FLIGHT SERIES 18 x 18, mixed media on canvas

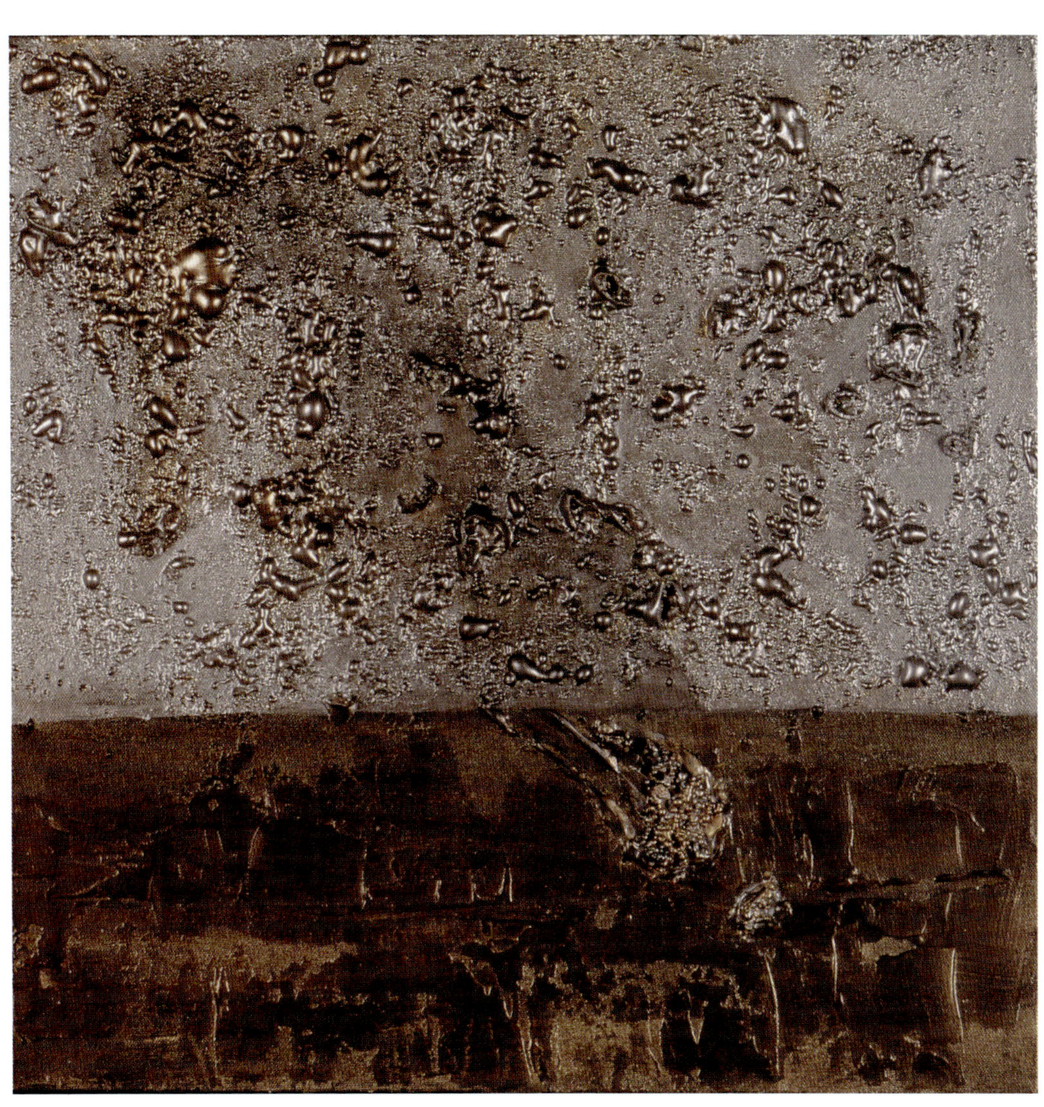

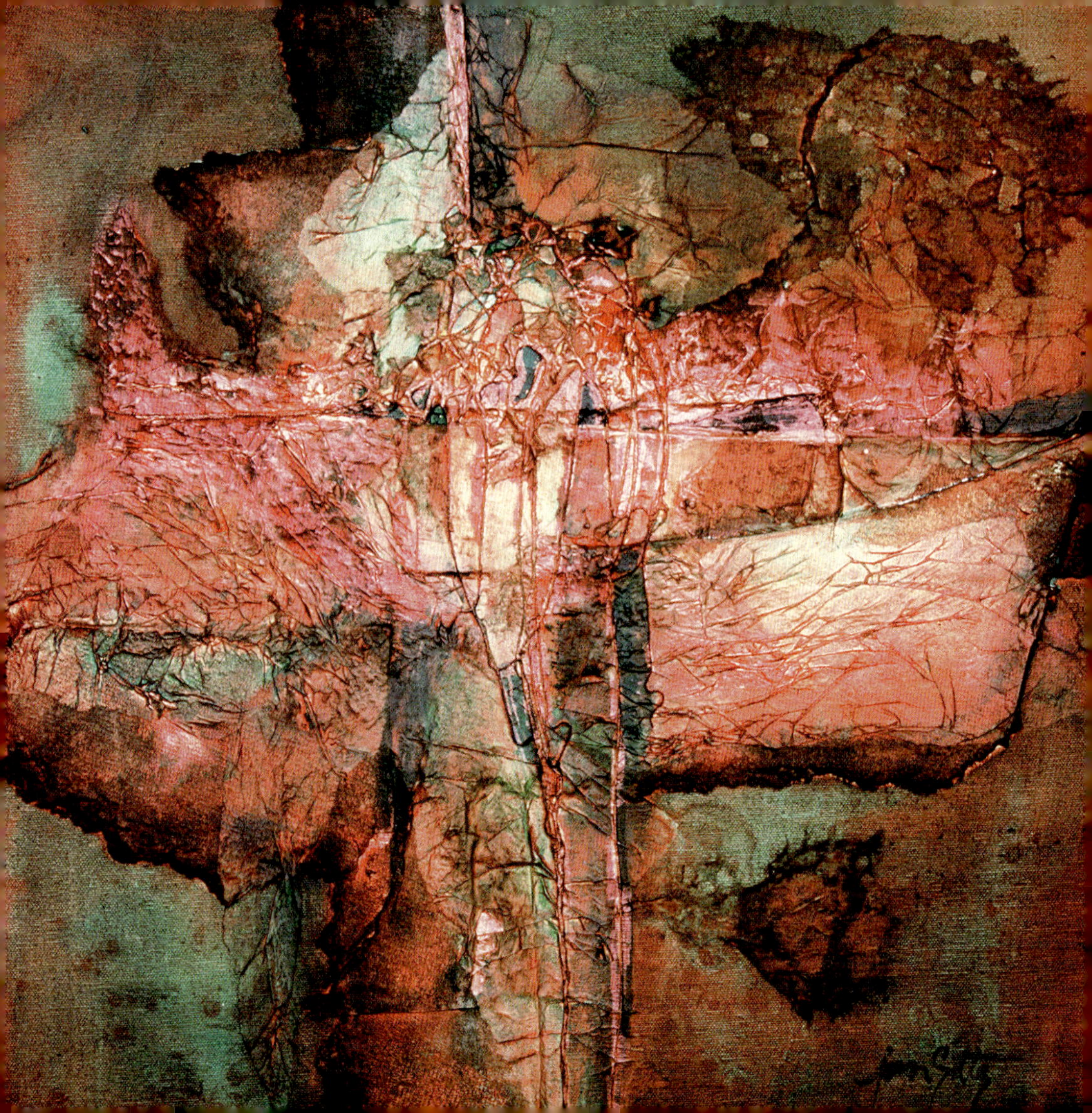

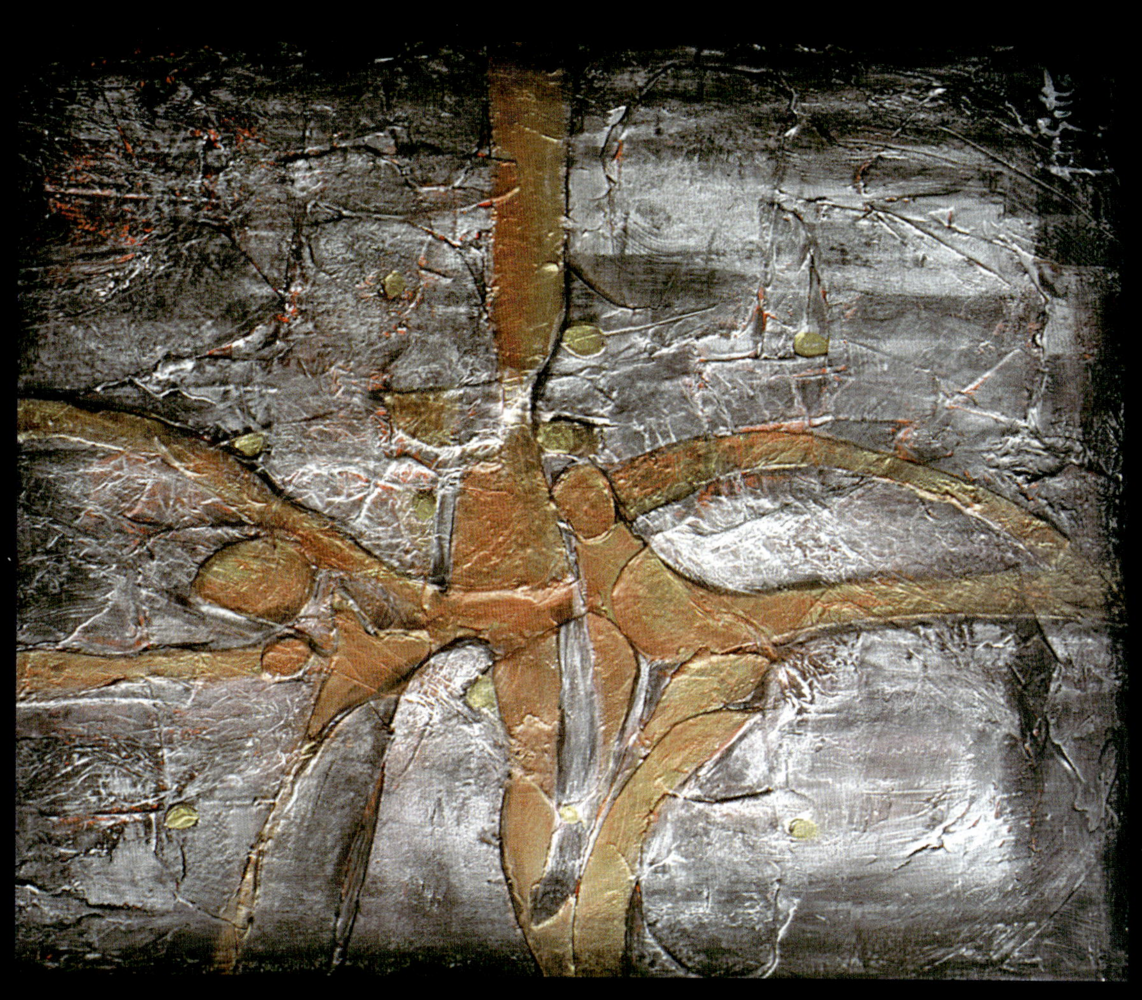

SONATA 24 x 36, mixed media on canvas

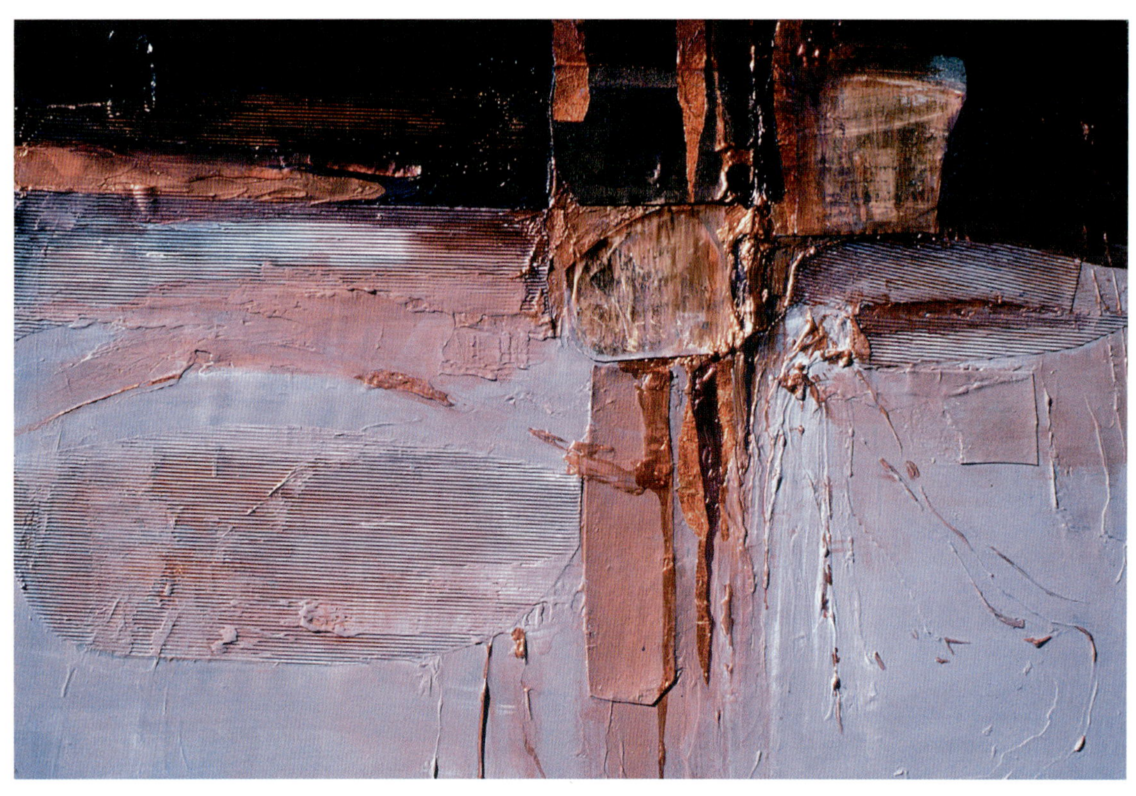

COPPER SUN 36 x 48, mixed media on canvas

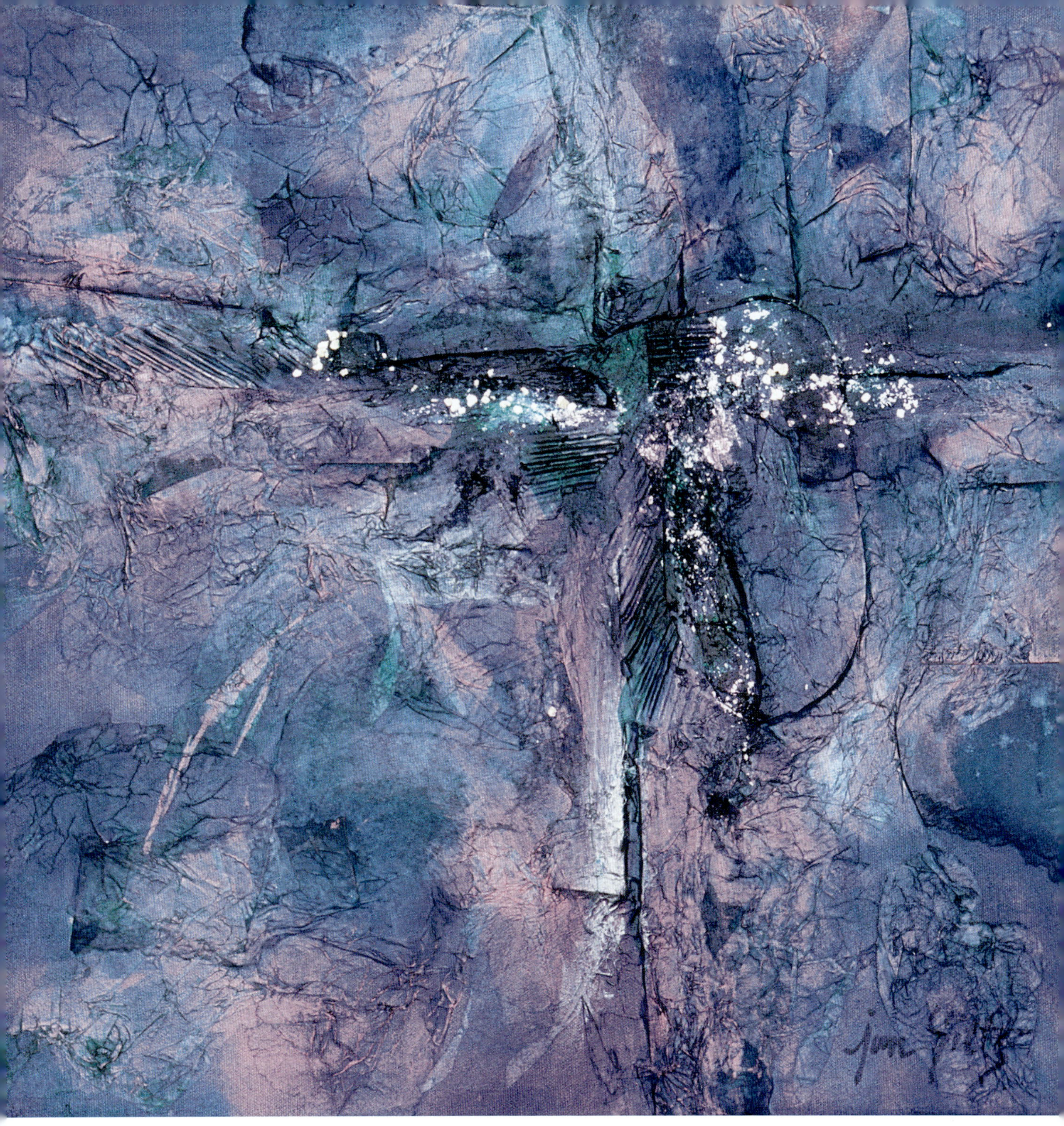

BLUE IN BLUE 18 x 18, mixed media on canvas

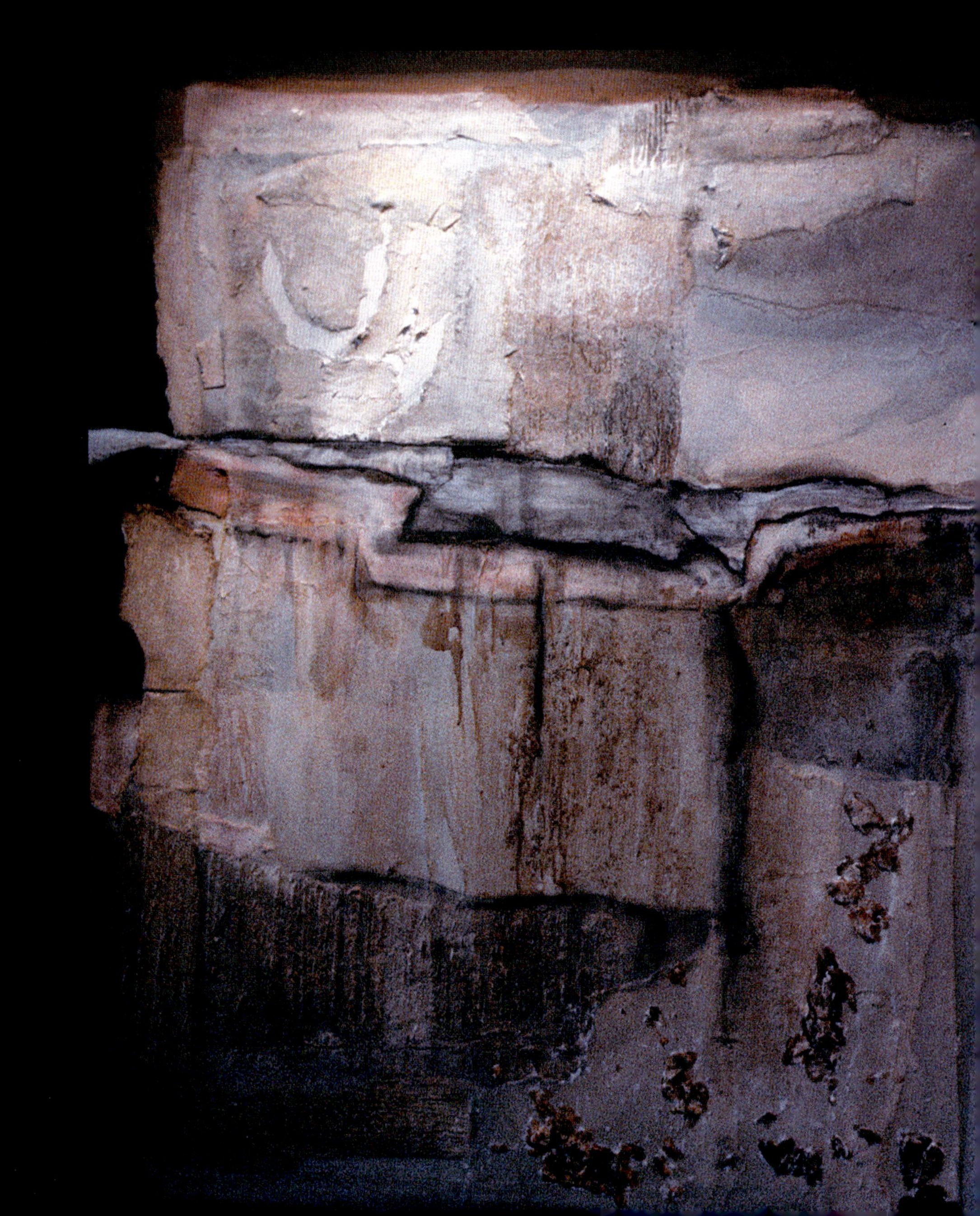

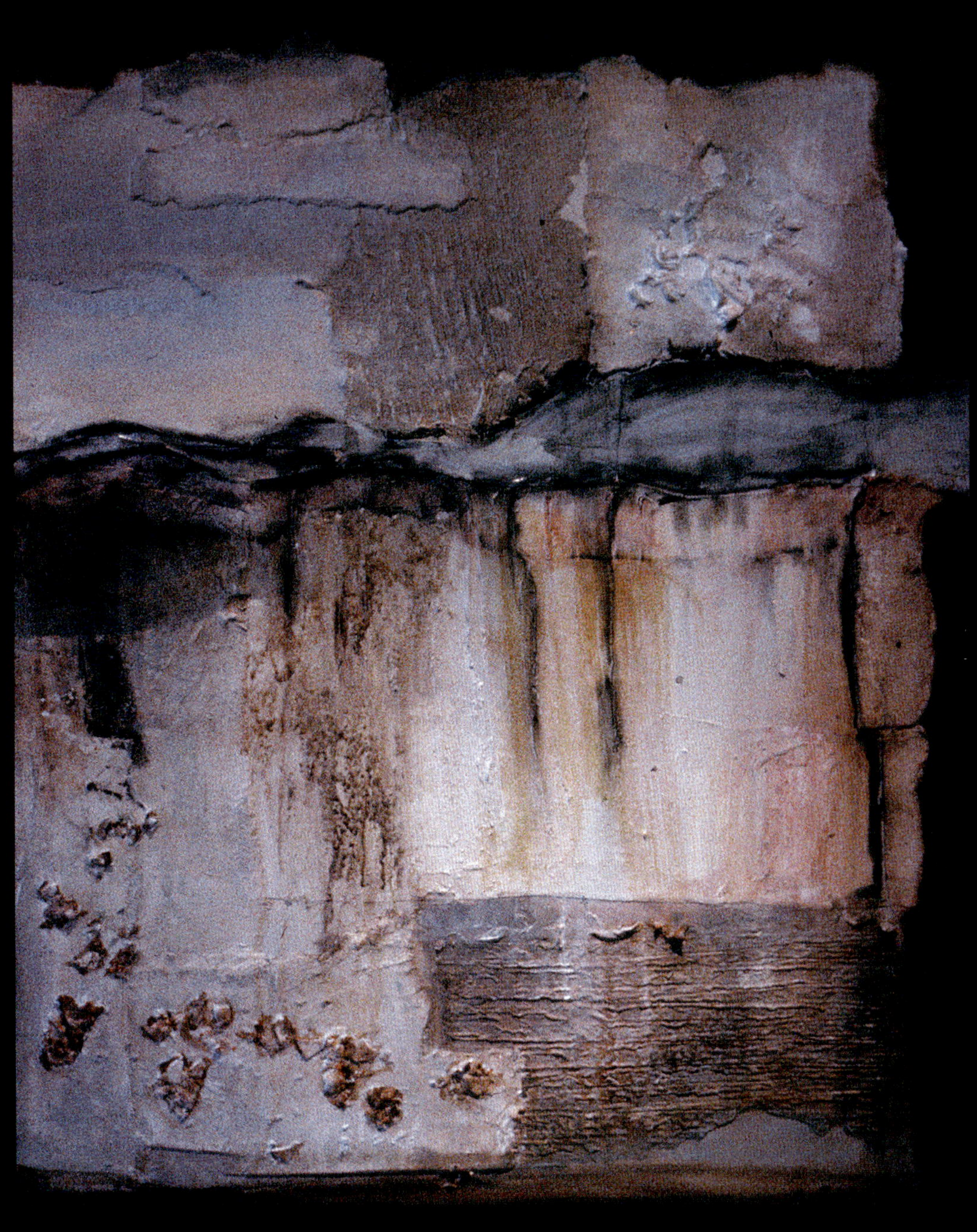

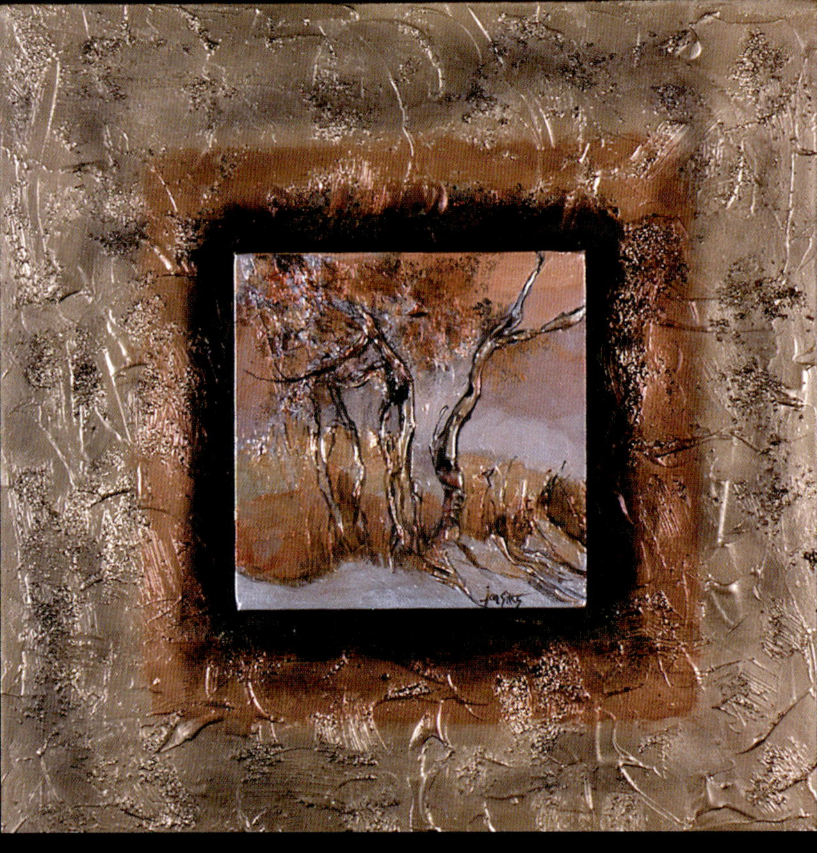

N GOLD

a on canvas

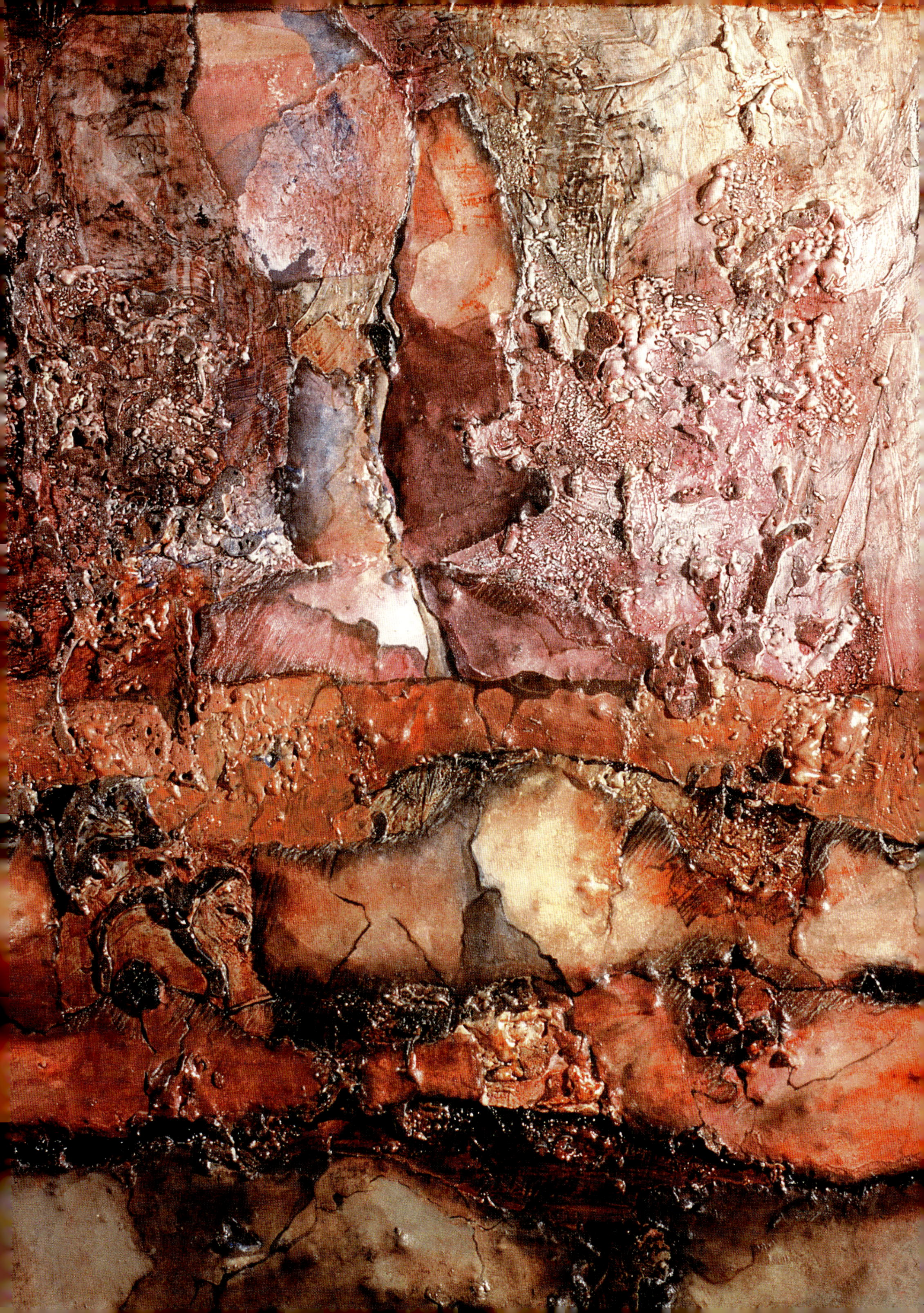

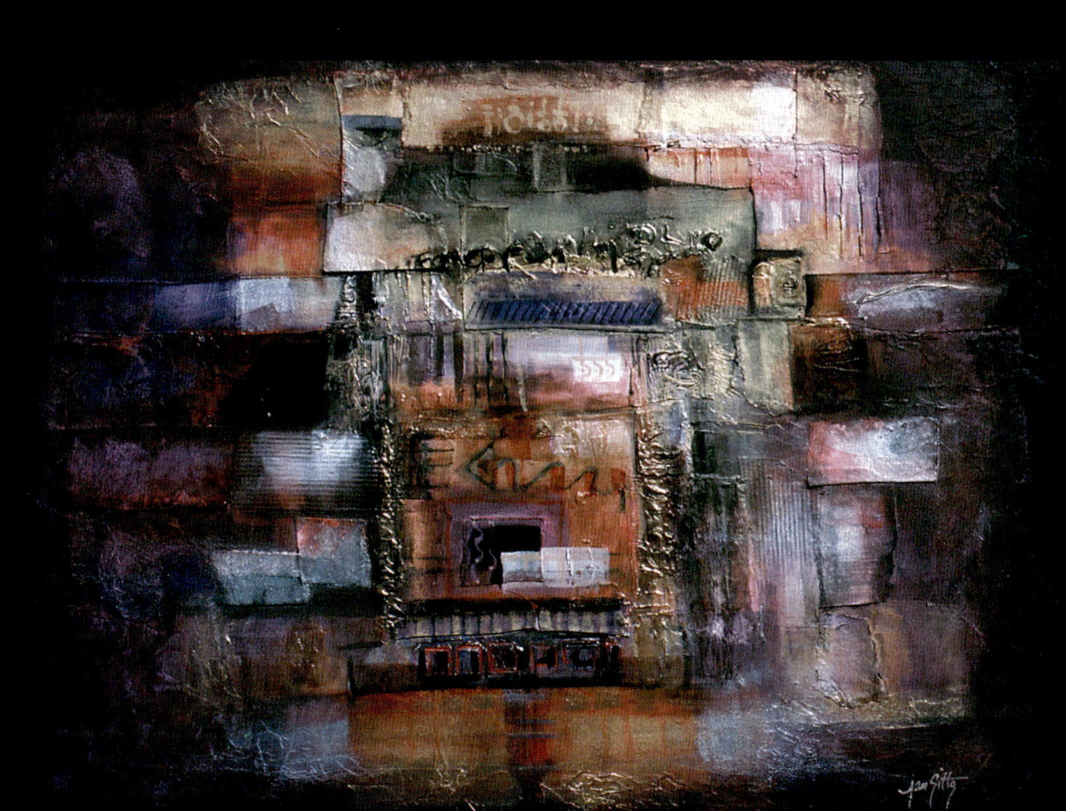

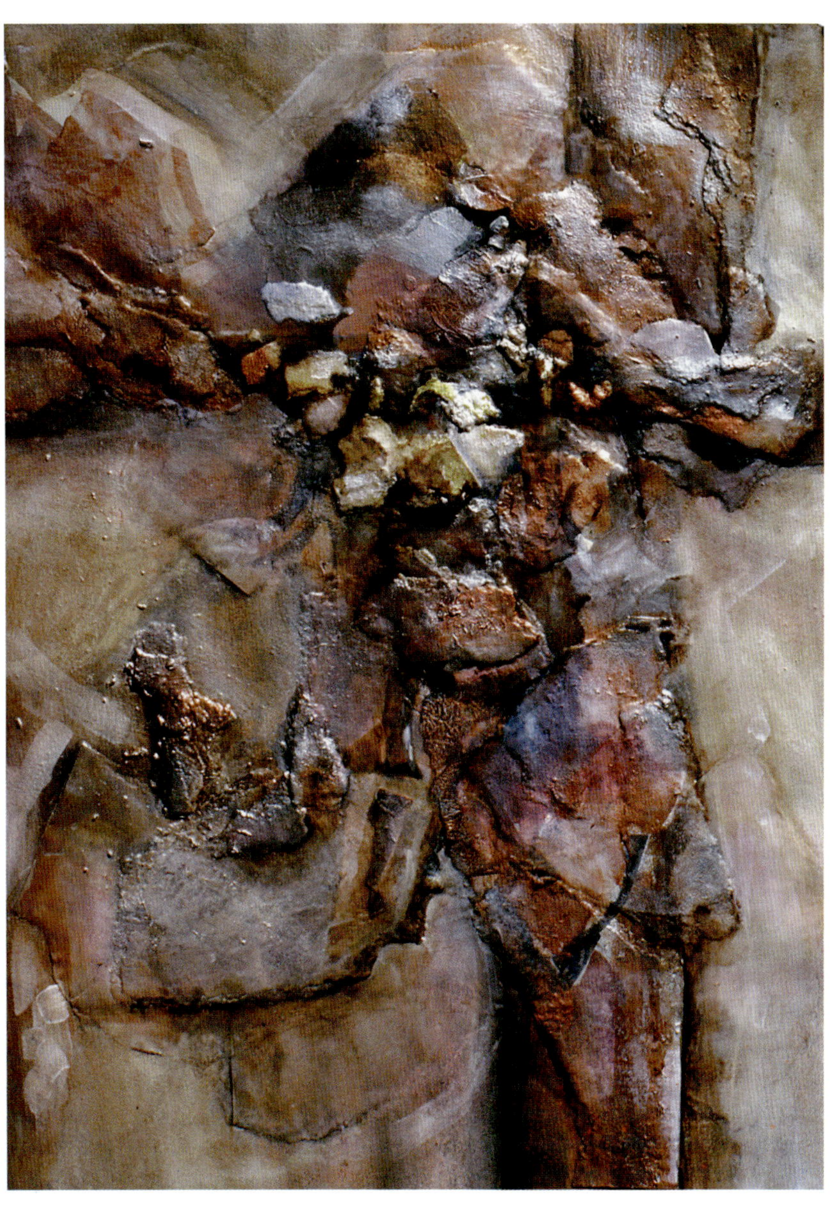

SEDONA SANDSTONE 30 x 40, mixed media on canvas

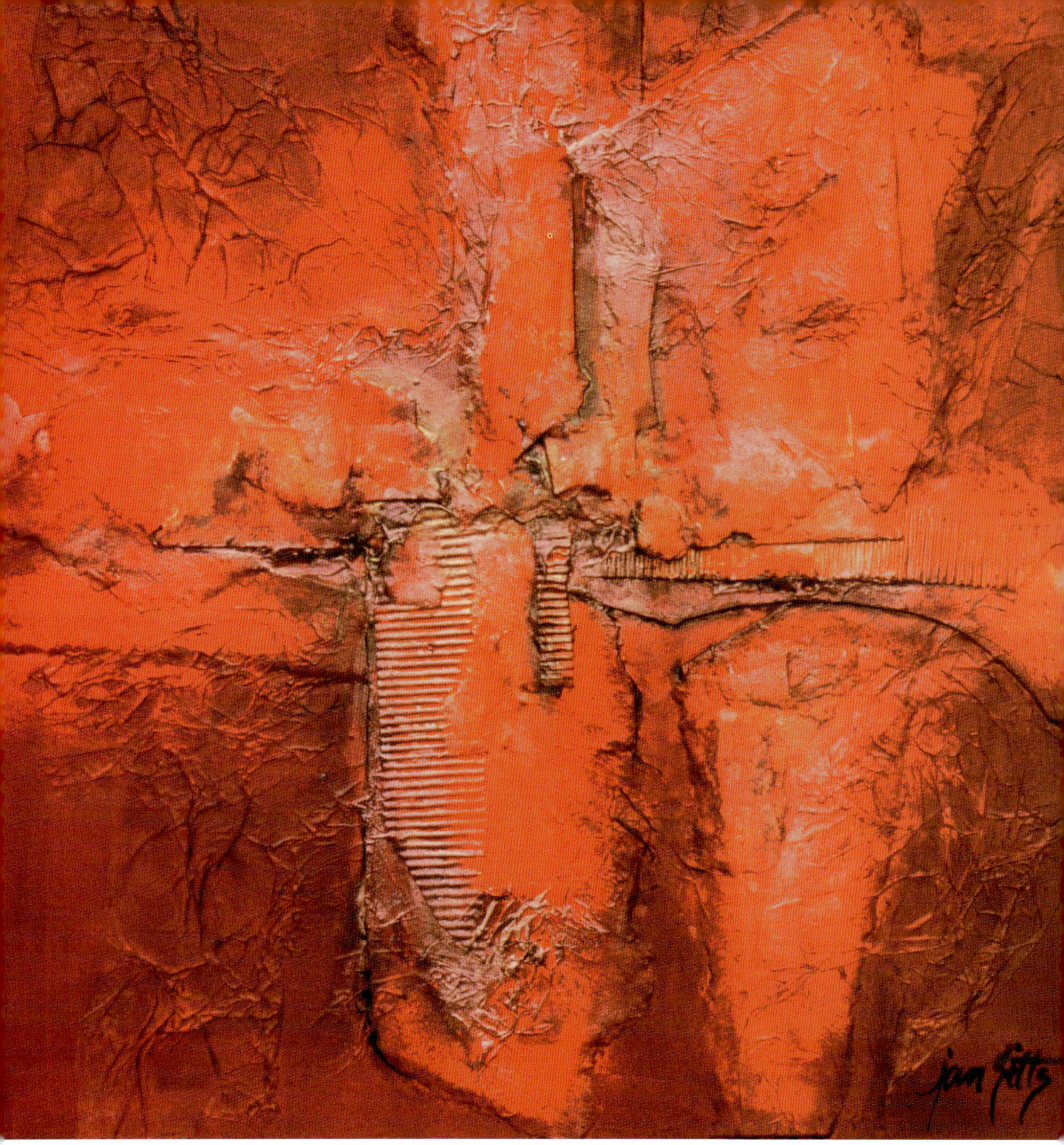

SEDONA RED 18 x 18, mixed media on canvas

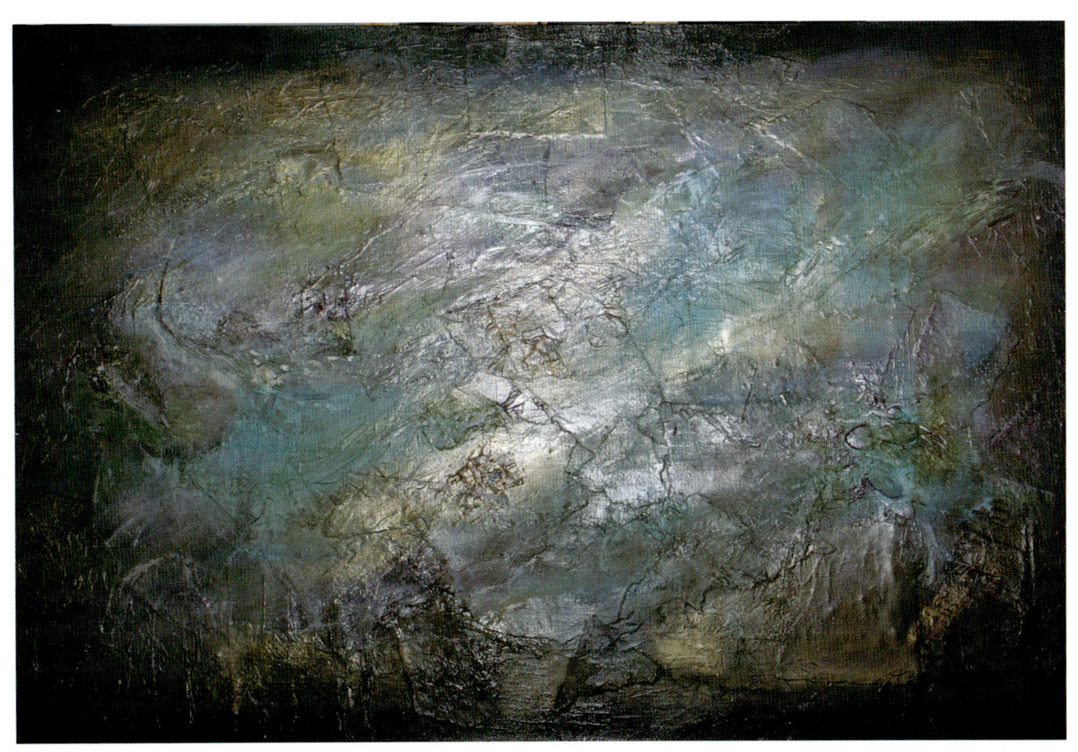

SEA SURFACE 24 x 36, mixed media on canvas

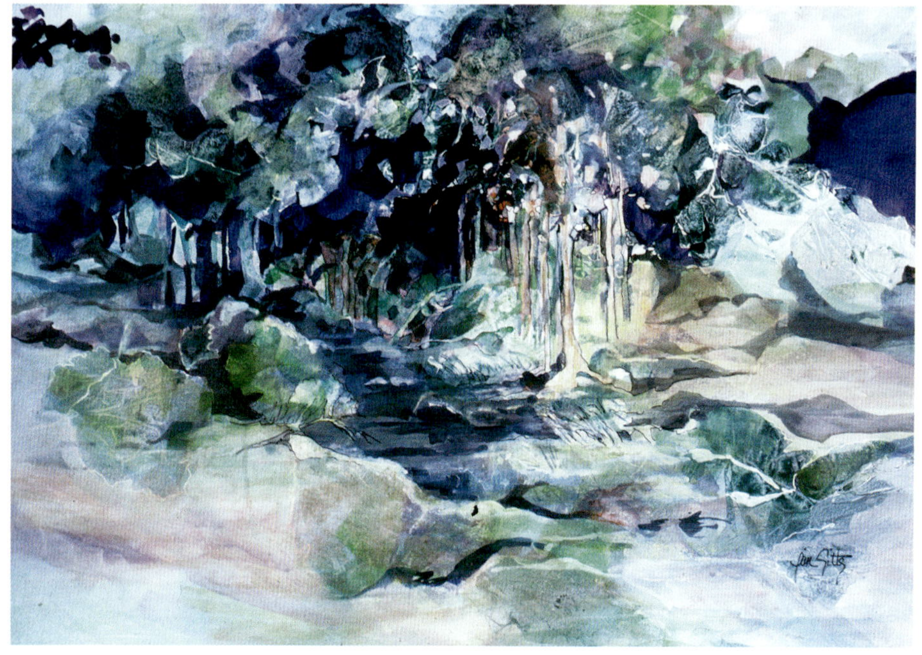

EVENING IMAGES 20 x 29, mixed media on canvas

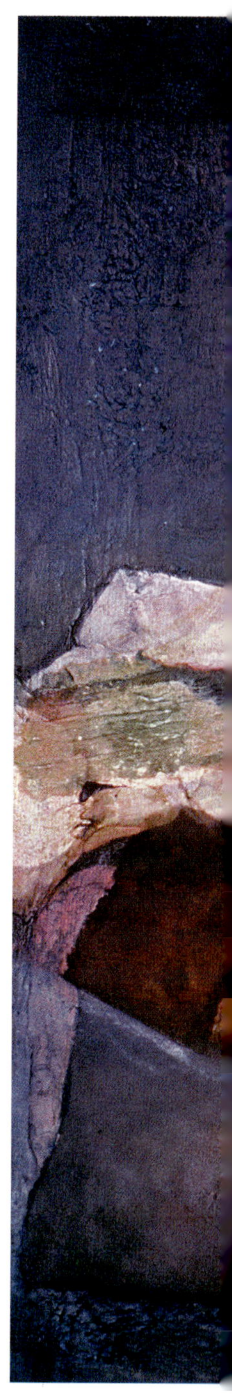

PAYDAR BLUE

30 x 40, mixed media on canvas

This piece is in the art collection of "Paydar" of Sedona, Arizona.

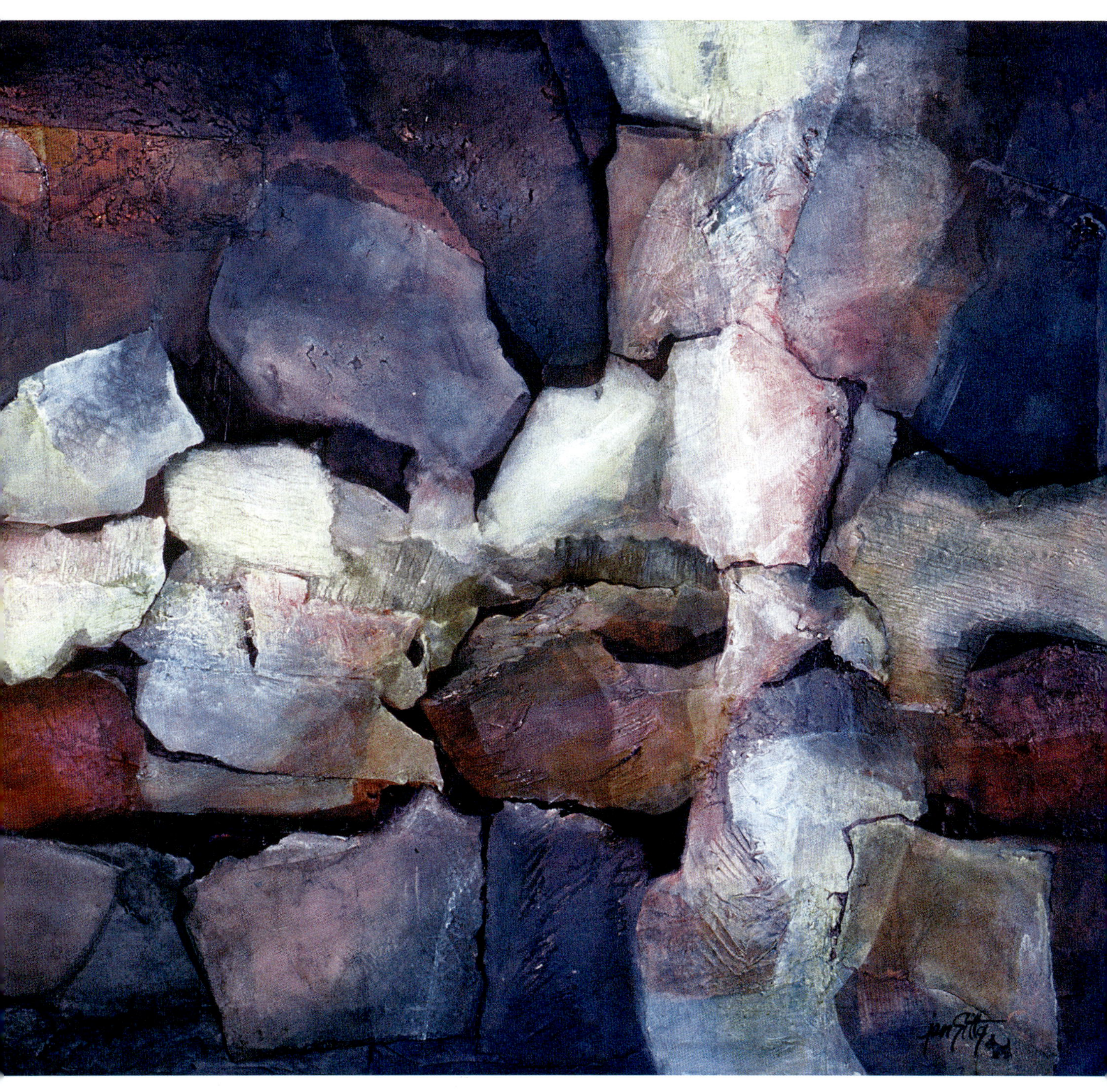

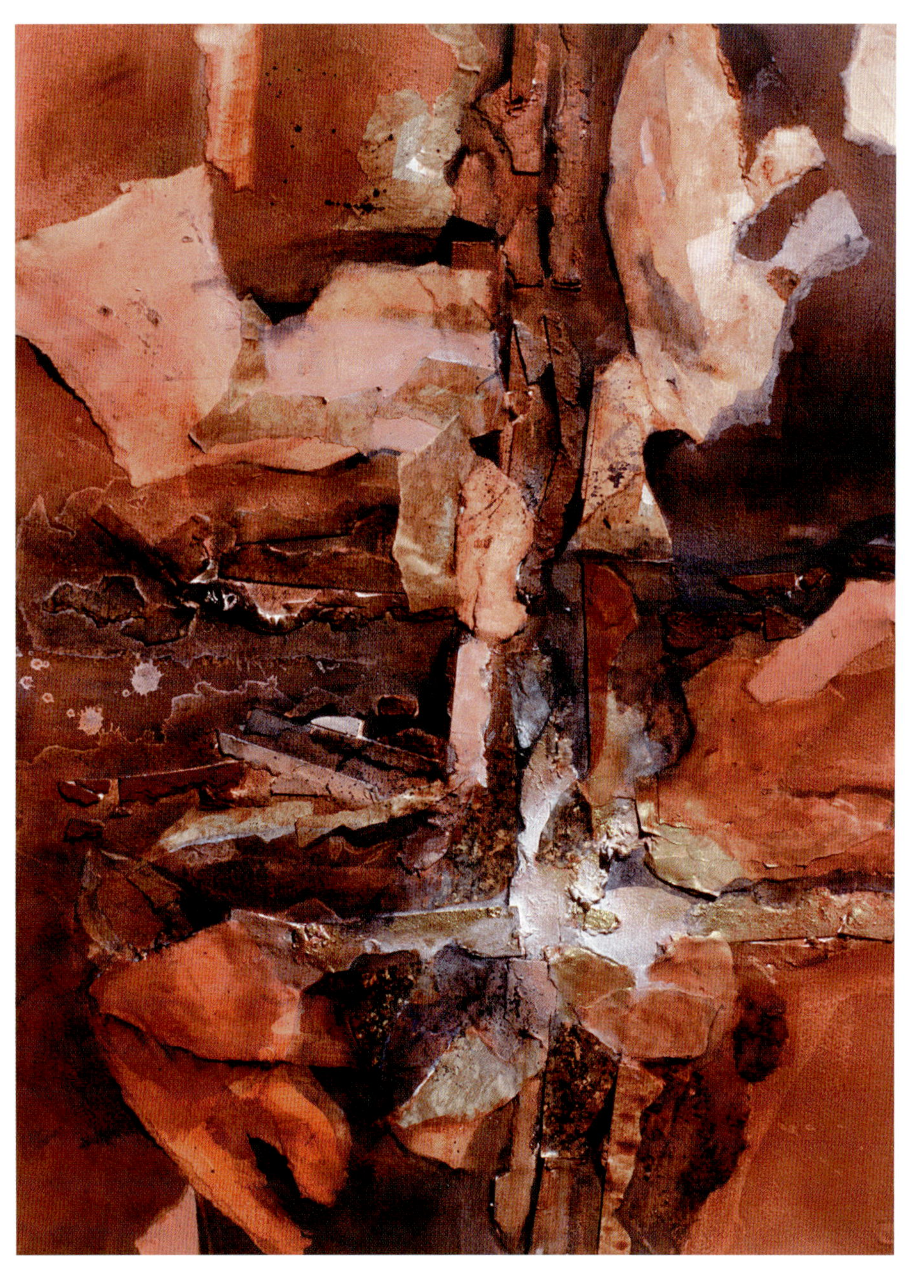

CANYON WATERS 22 x 36, mixed media on canvas

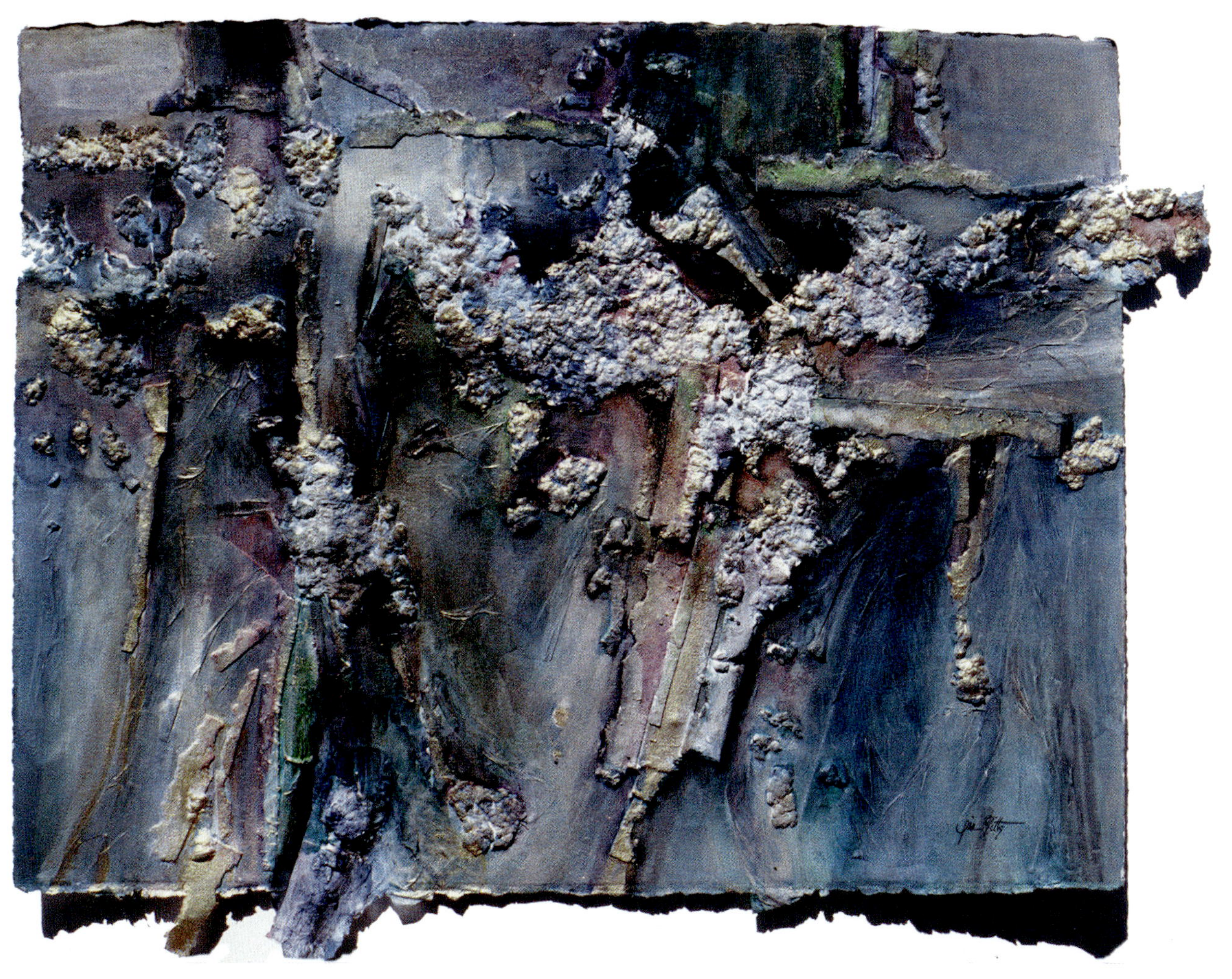

DANCING WATERS 22 x 30, mixed media on canvas

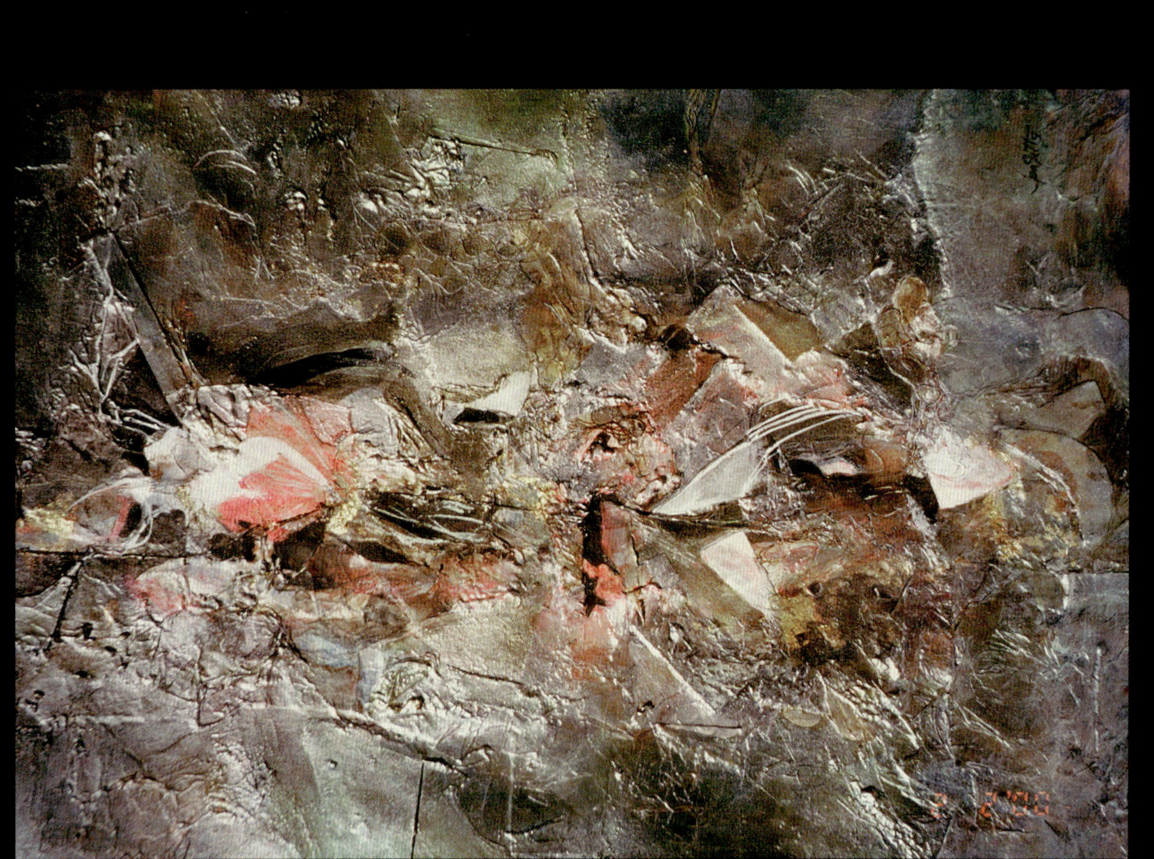

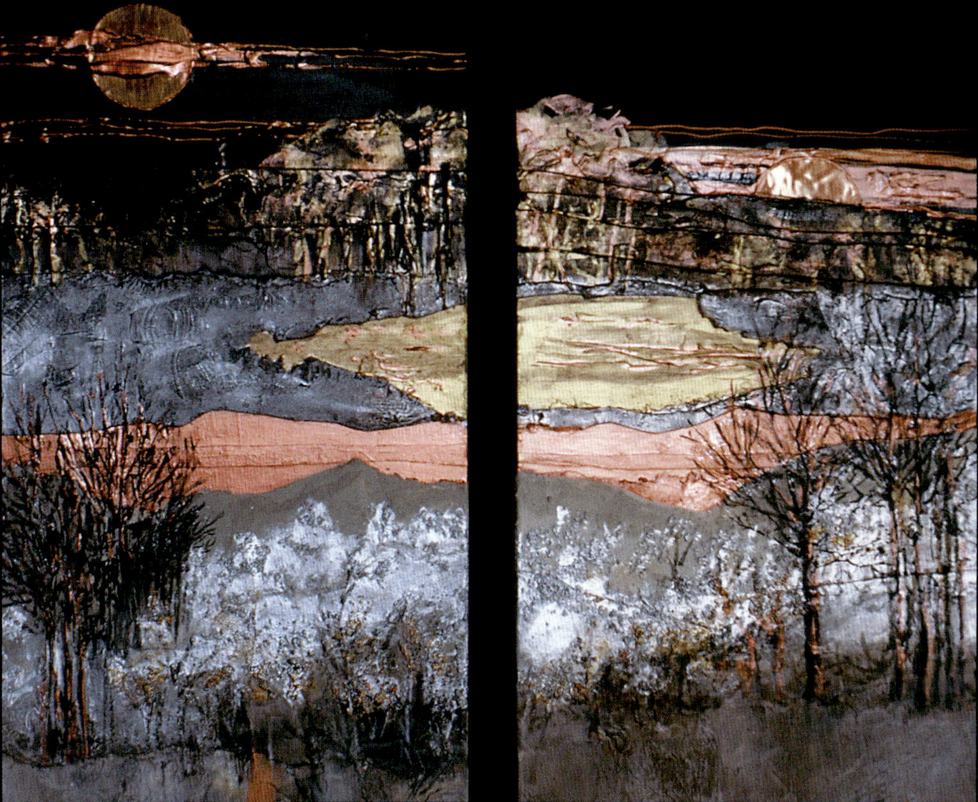

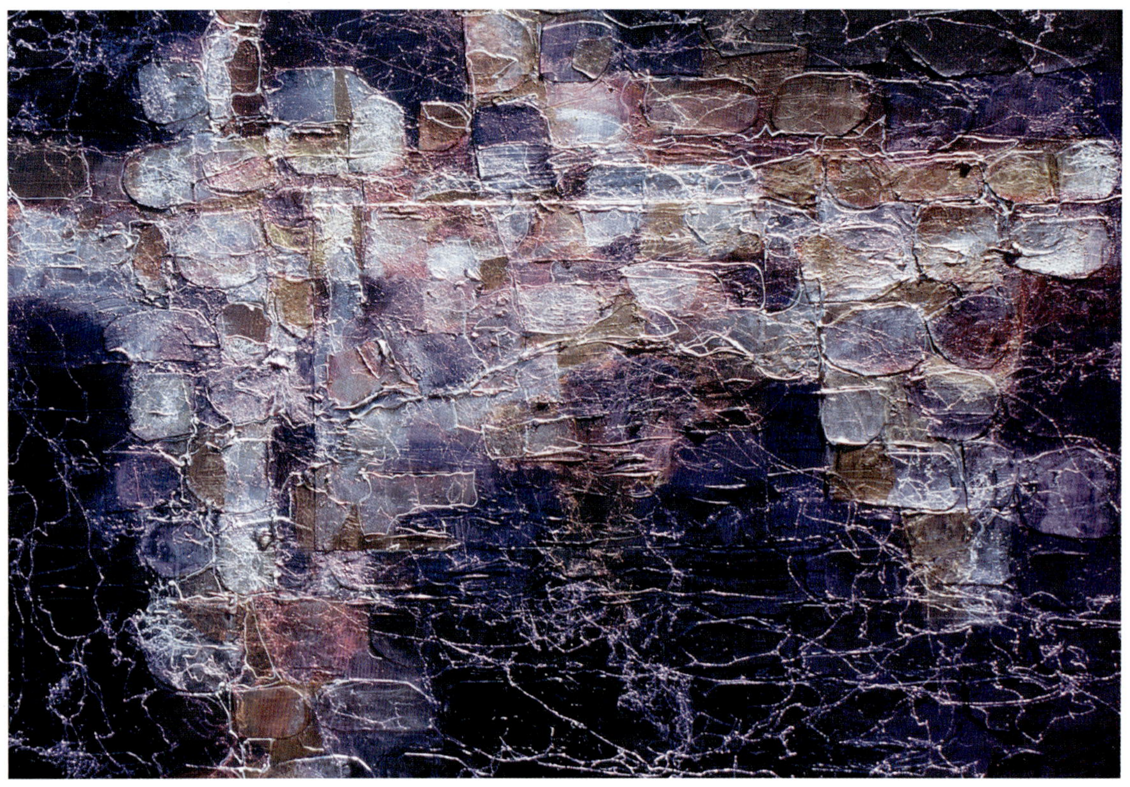

SILVER THREADS

30 x 40, mixed media on canvas

In 2001 I became Arizona's state district coordinator for the Society of Layerists in Multi-Media. I wanted to paint an impression of the inner spirit and how we are all interconnected through our art. These silver threads linked symbolically to one another cross a shape suggesting the United States in my visualization of the SLMM philosophy.

REFLECTIONS (DETAIL)

36 x 48, mixed media on canvas

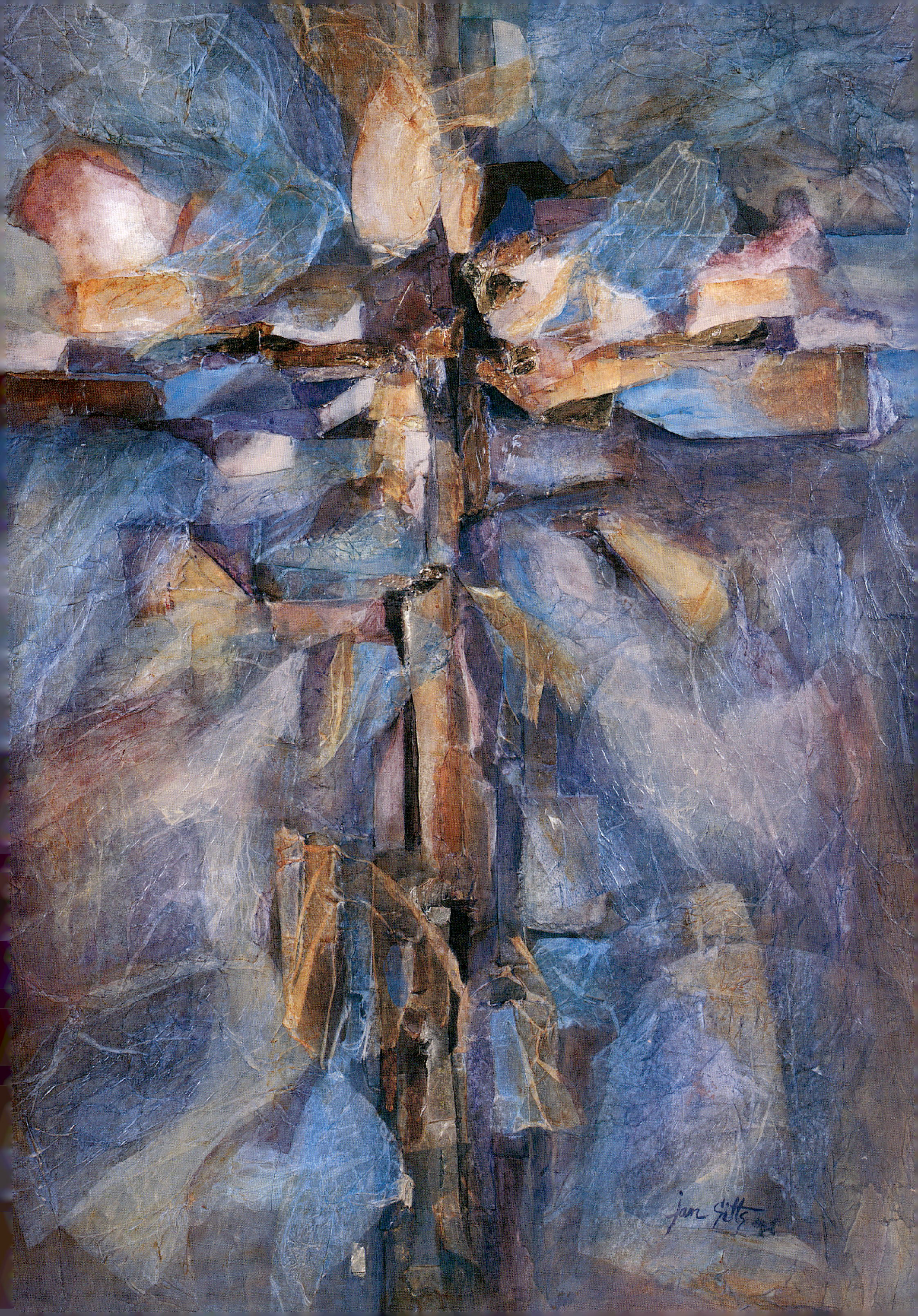

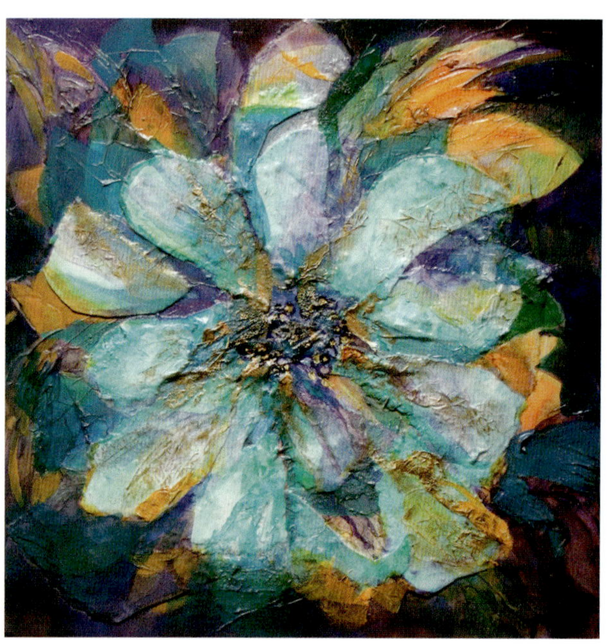

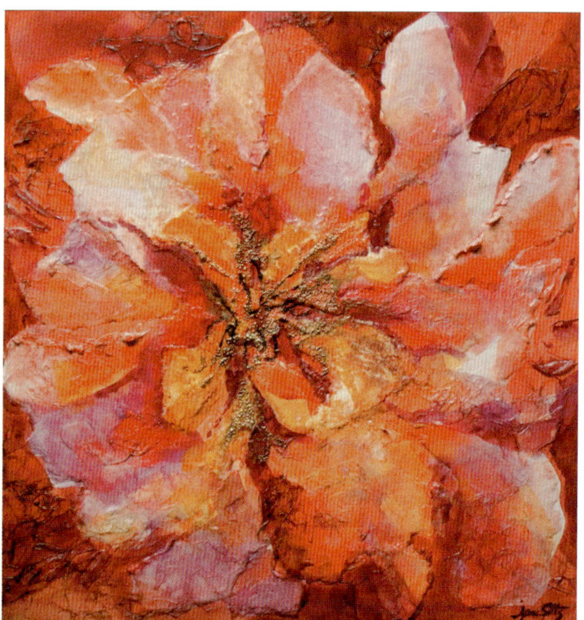

BLUE FLOWER, RED FLOWER, PINK FLOWER Each 18 x 18, mixed media on canvas

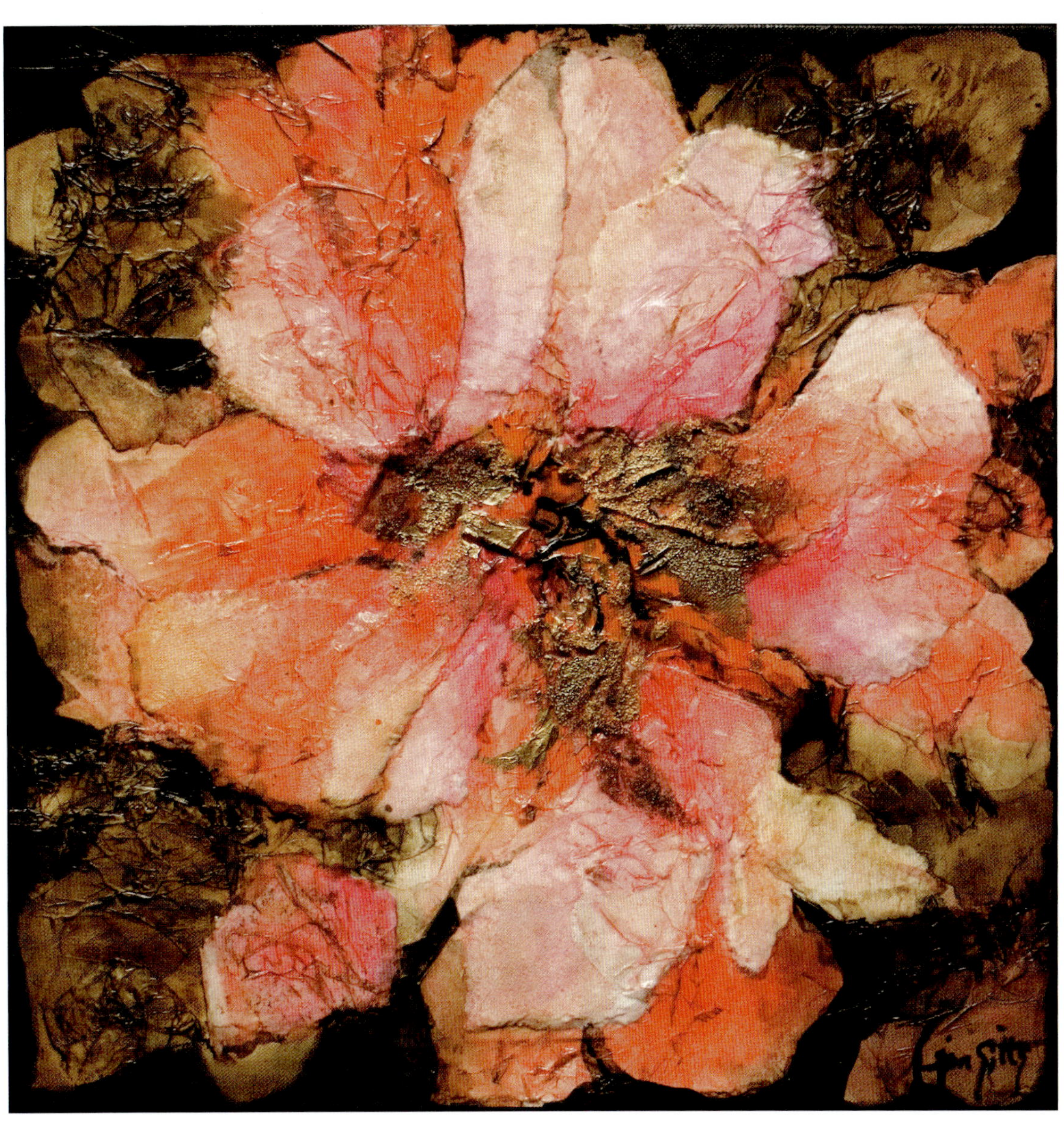

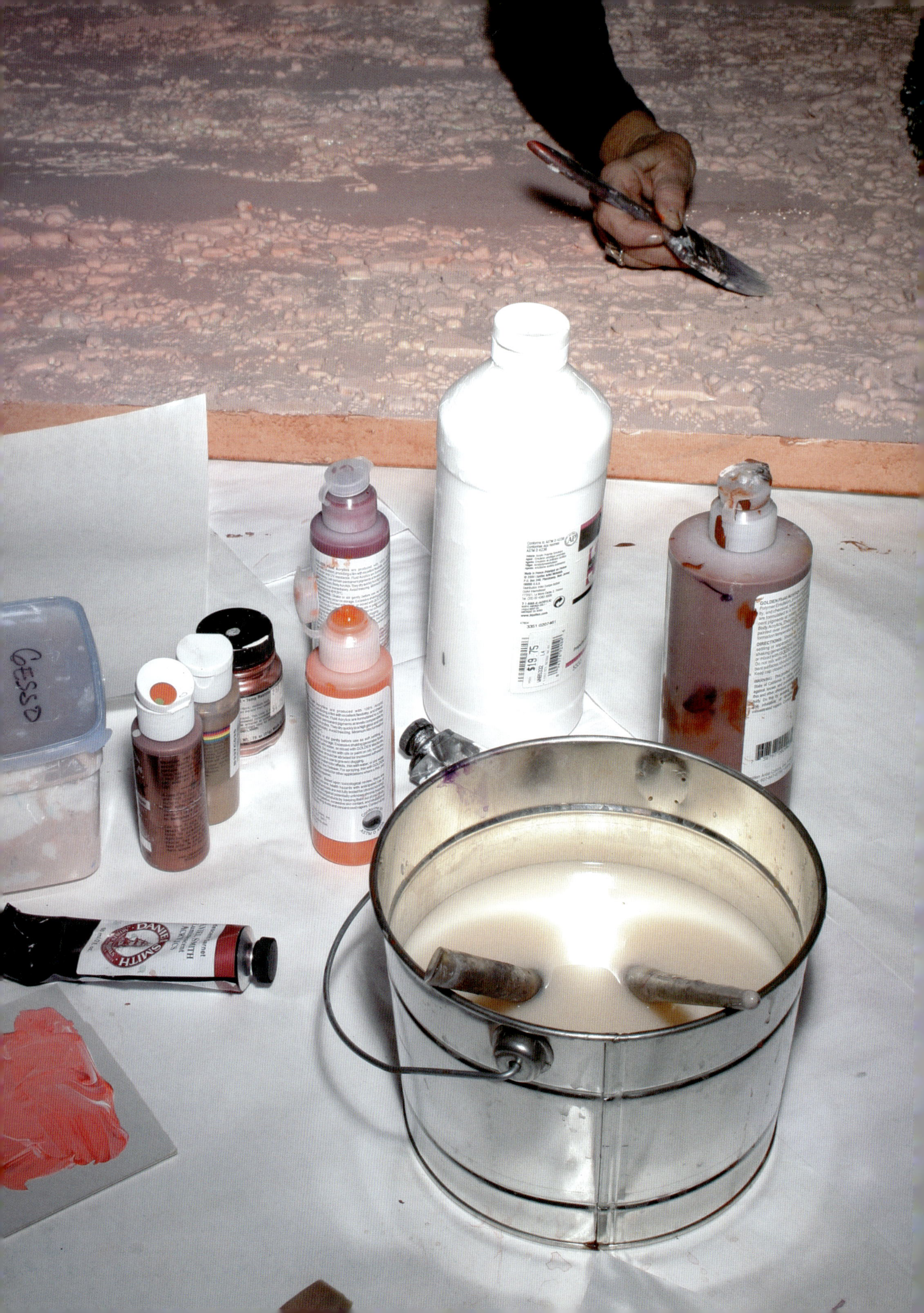
GESSO
DANIEL SMITH
$19.75

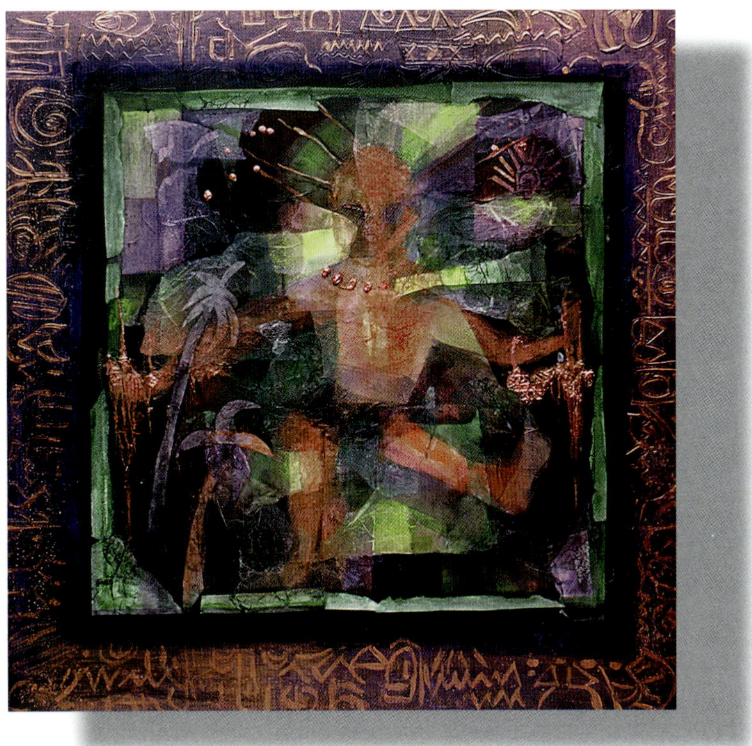

C O S T A   R I C A   36 x 36, mixed media on canvas

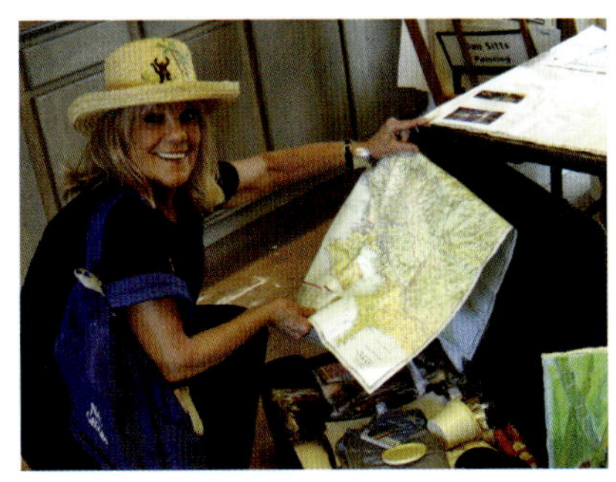

I took a group to Costa Rica on one of my many painting workshops, and to say the least, this was a most rewarding experience to students and teacher alike. We were on the Peninsula de Osa, in the heart of a remote jungle preserve. The weather was hot and humid but the students and I managed to paint some of our best work. This country enlightened my senses — the sounds, colors, animals and the whole experience.

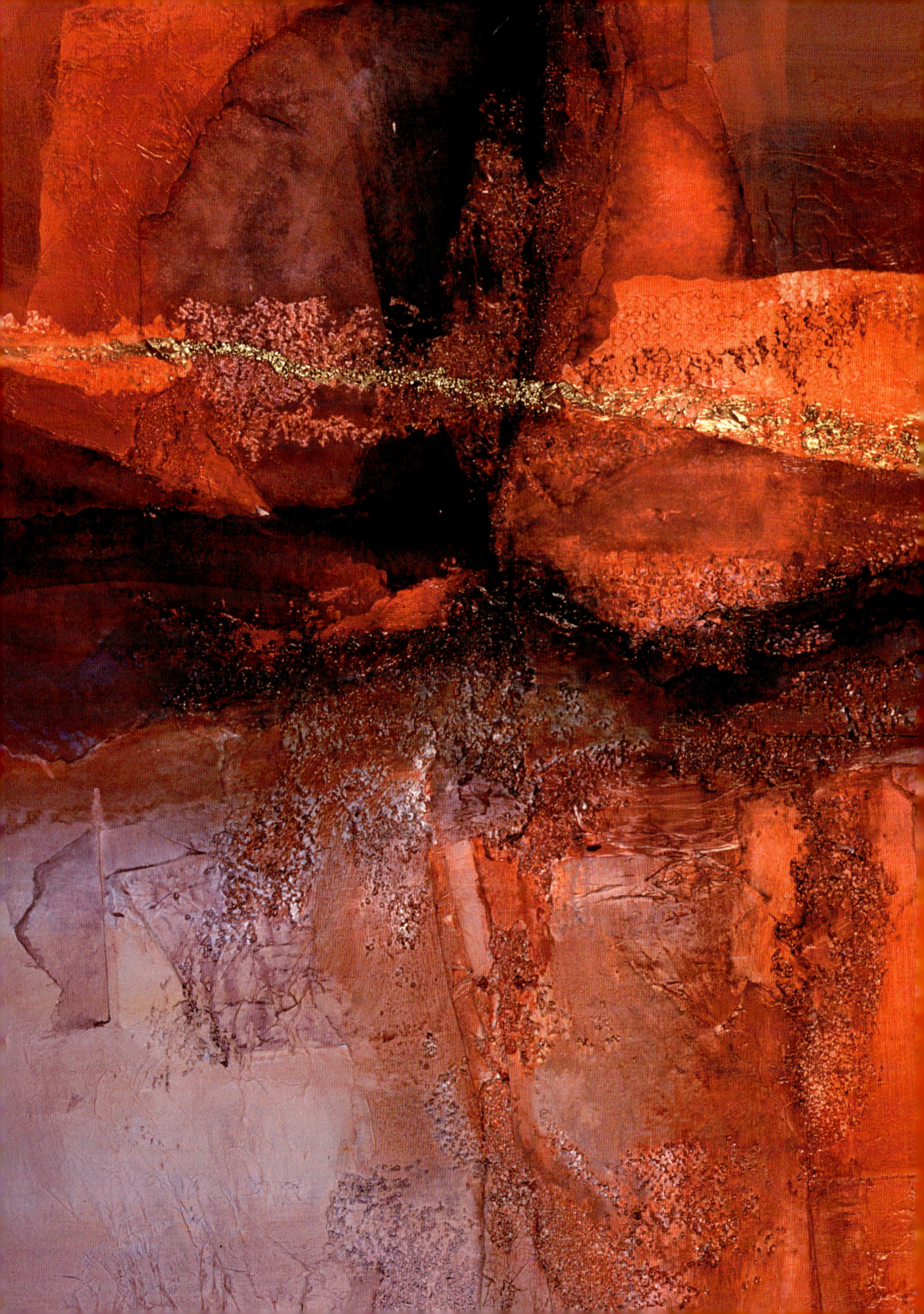

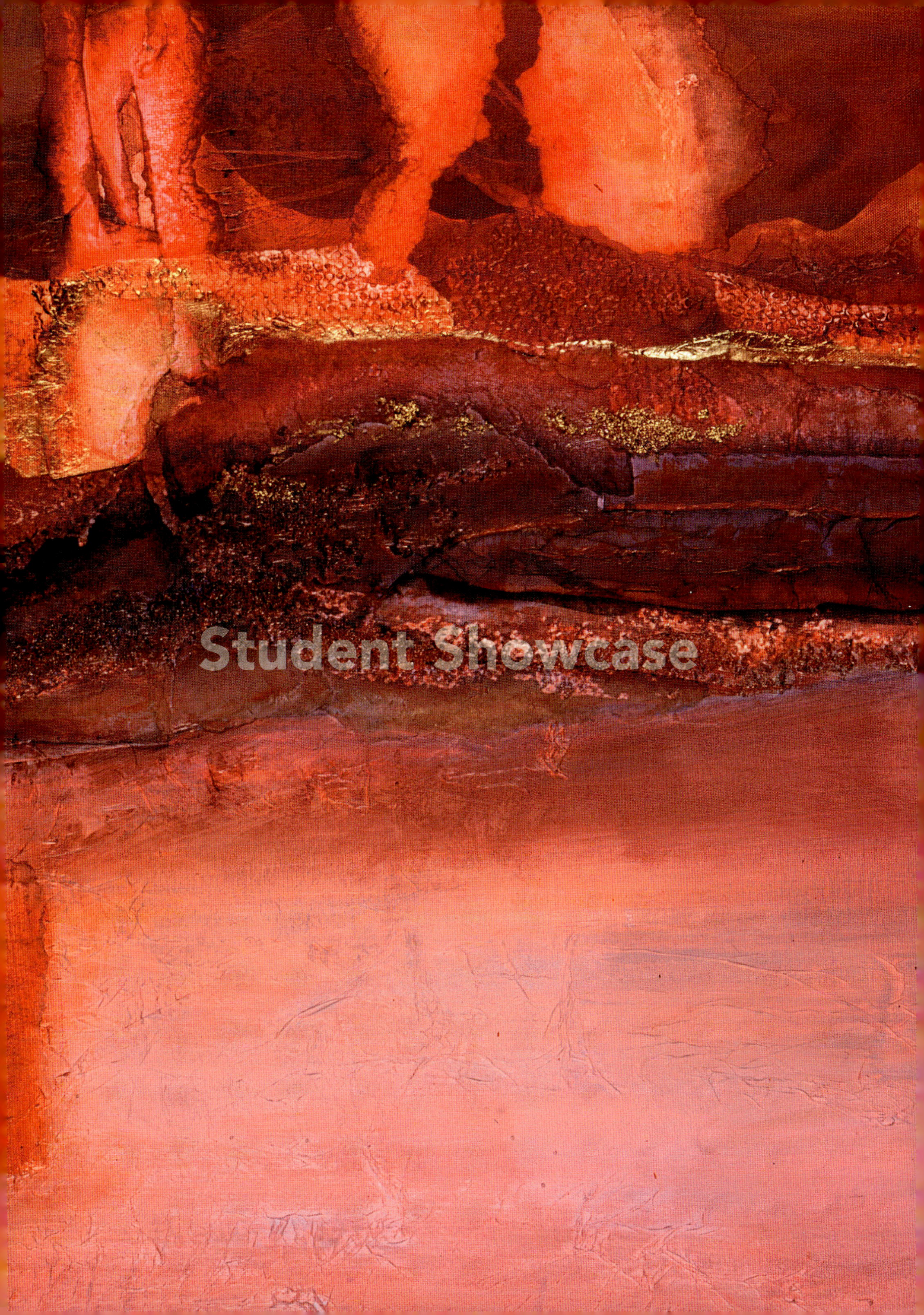
Student Showcase

STUDENT SHOWCASE

Teaching is a big part of my life and I am always thrilled at what my workshop participants accomplish. Here is a small sampling of fine work by participants in my workshops.

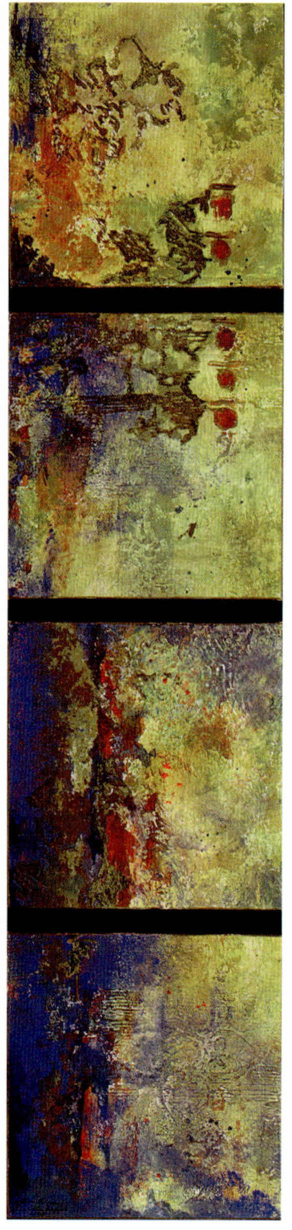

CYNTHIA ADAMS, FL

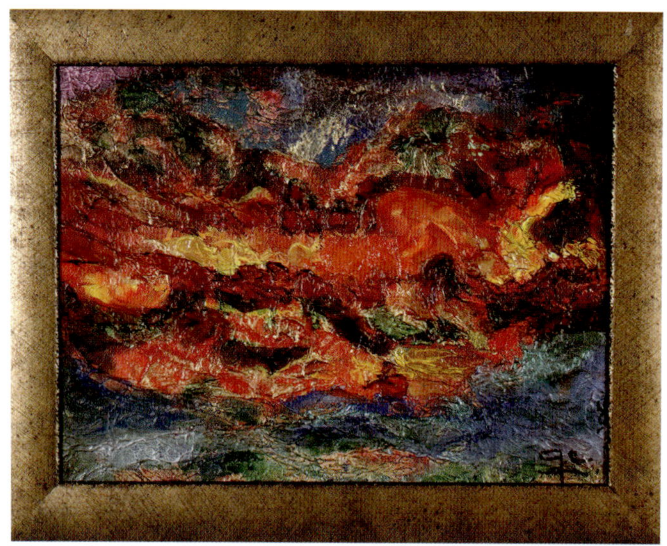

FR. J.C. ORTIZ, AZ

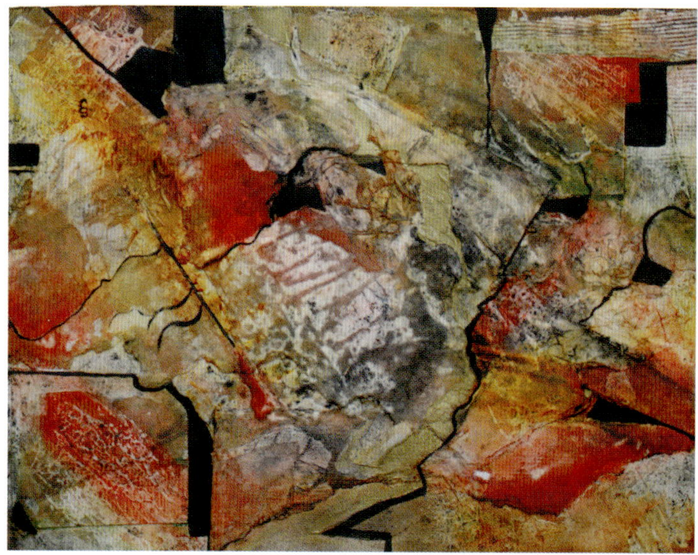

SHARON JENKINS, FL

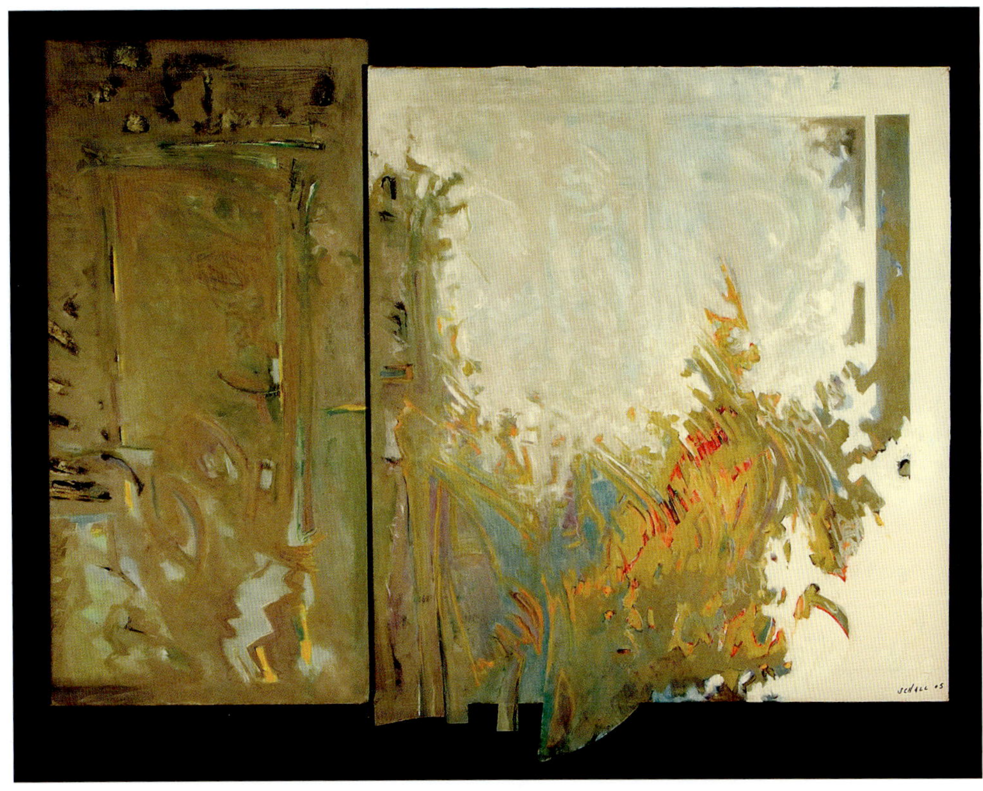

KEITH SCHALL, AZ

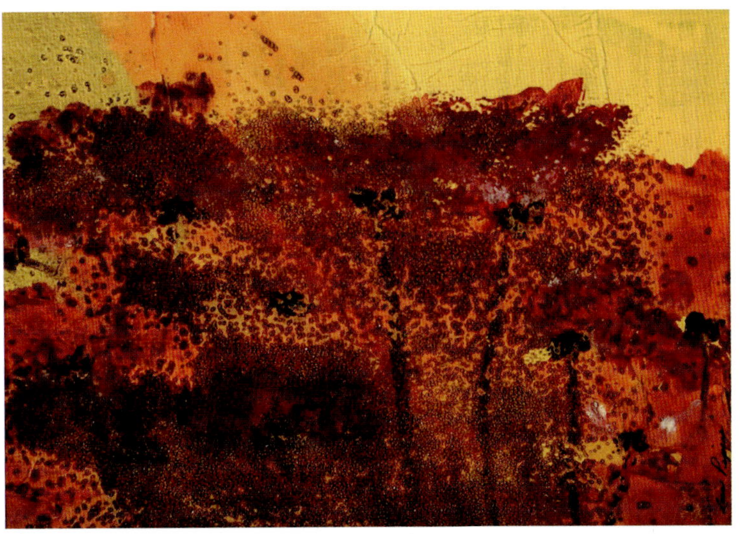

LOIS PEPINO, AZ

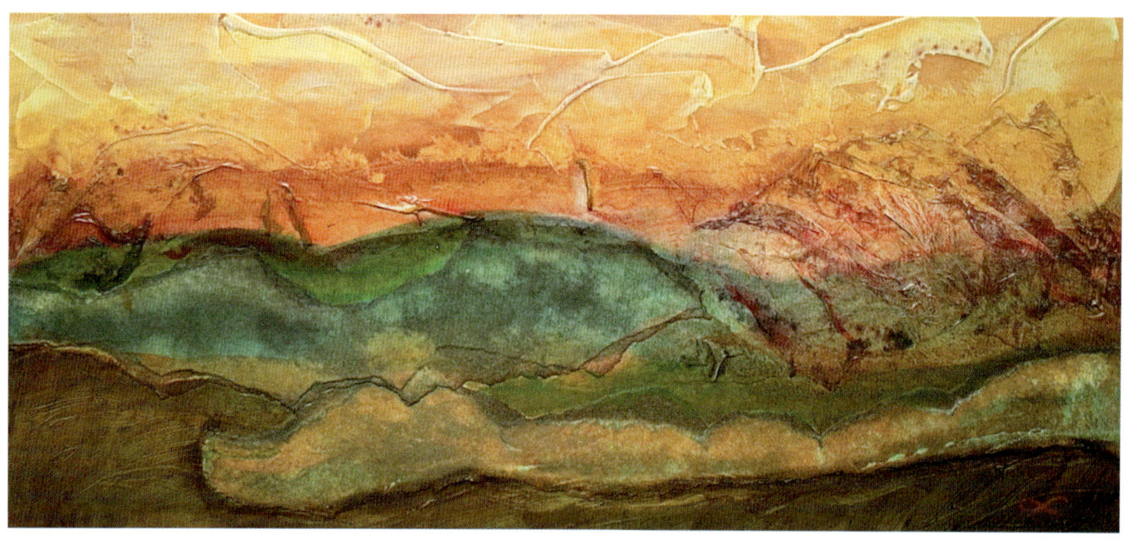

LORRAINE ROMANK, CANADA

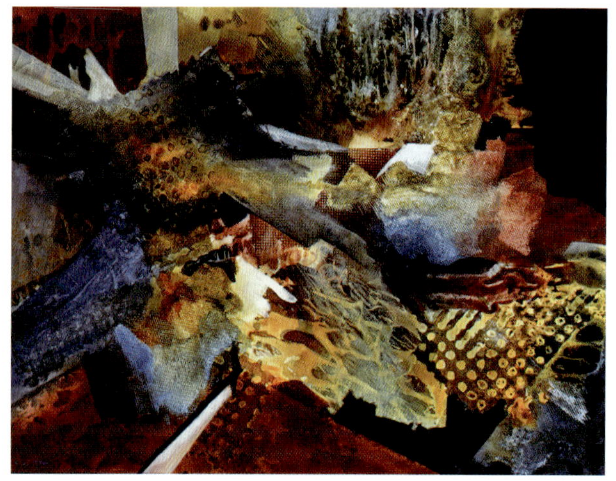

LOIS MACDONALD, AZ

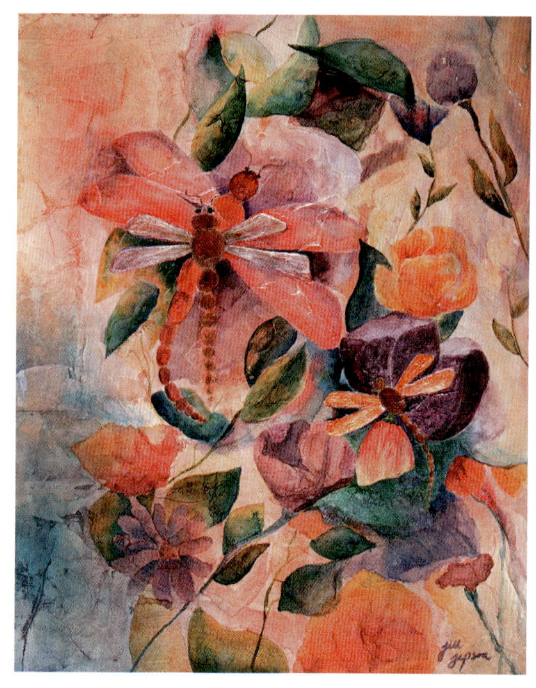

JILL JEPSON, AZ

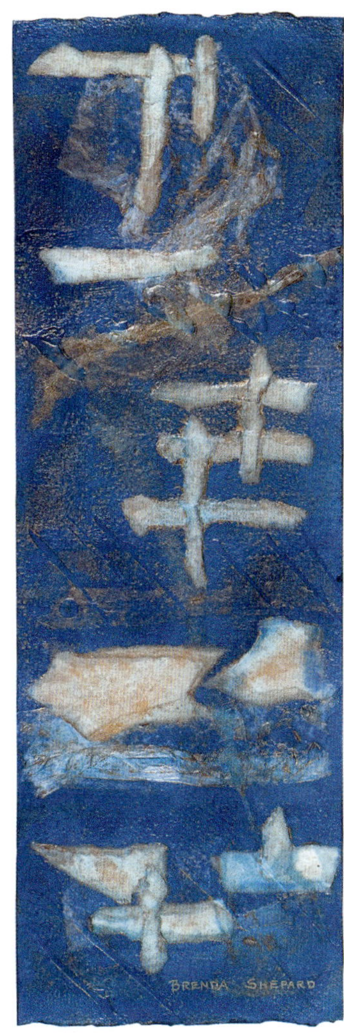

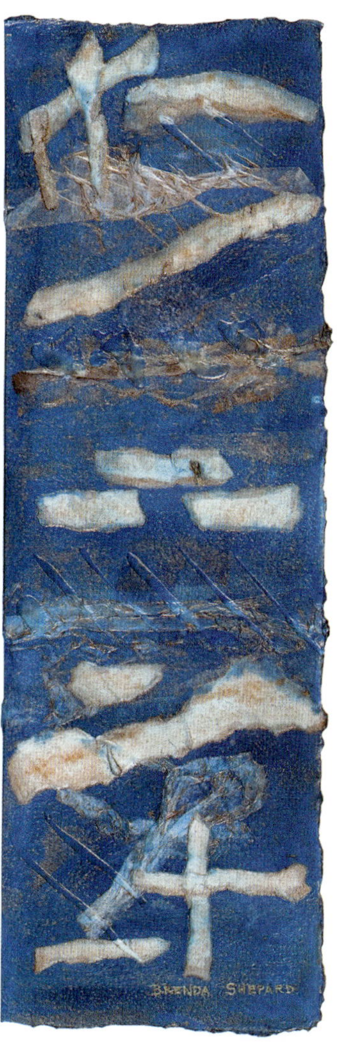

BRENDA SHEPARD, CA

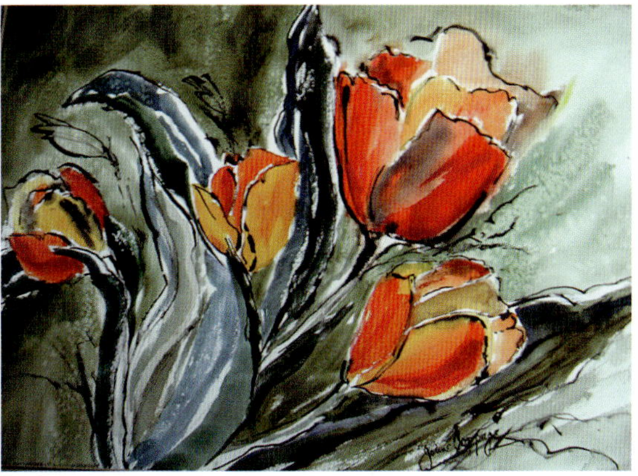

JODINE BROSCOVAK, CO

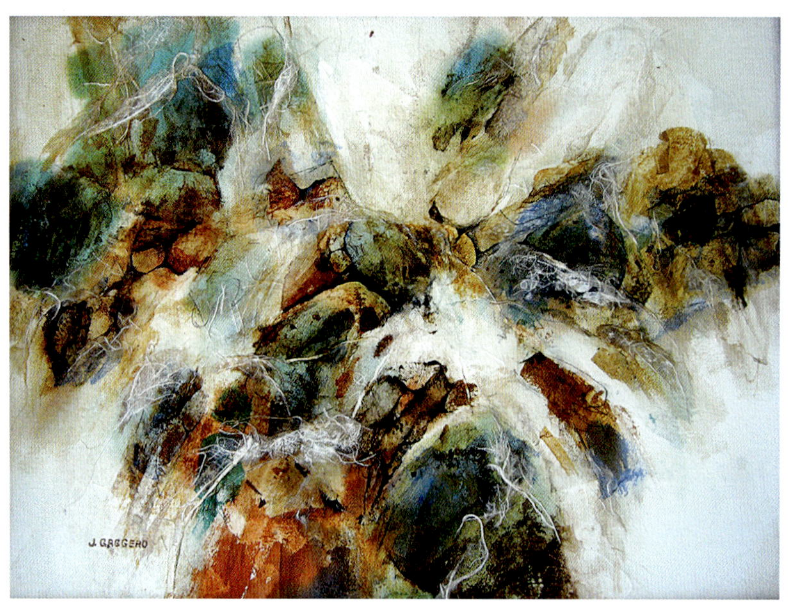

JUDY GAGGERO, FL

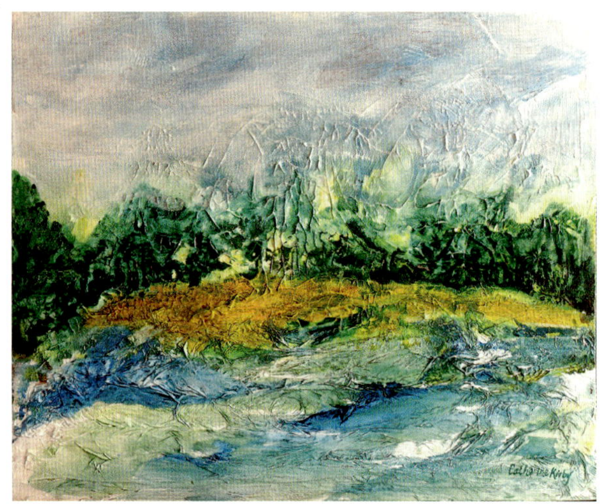

CATHERINE KIRBY, PA

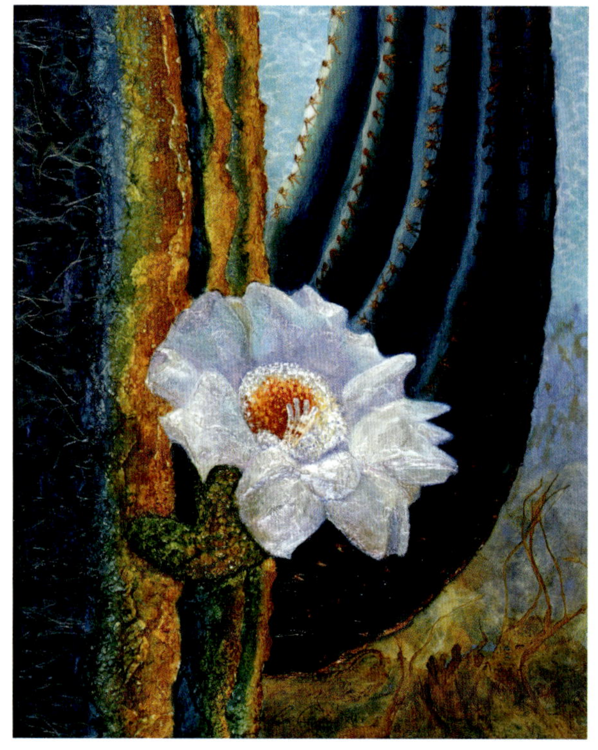

RUTH CANADA, AZ